TRANSFORMING THE
OPERATING ROOM

INNOVATIVE LEADERSHIP STRATEGIES FOR SURGICAL EFFICIENCY

DESIGNED FOR HEALTHCARE
PROFESSIONALS & STUDENTS

TRANSFORMING THE
OPERATING ROOM

INNOVATIVE LEADERSHIP STRATEGIES FOR SURGICAL EFFICIENCY

DESIGNED FOR HEALTHCARE PROFESSIONALS & STUDENTS

SUMIT SHARMA
MBA, MBB, SCPM, CHFP

DEDICATION

To my parents, **Mr. V. N. Sharma, I.P.S.,** and **Prof. Dr. Meena Sharma,** whose unwavering love and guidance have been the foundation of my journey.

To my dad for teaching me discipline and perseverance.

To my mom for instilling in me the values of compassion and service.

To my wife, **Deepti Sharma,** for being my rock, partner, and constant encouragement.

To my children, **Savar, Saesha,** and **Vyom Sharma,** who inspire me daily to dream bigger and strive for excellence.

To my brother, **Varun Sharma,** and my sister, **Dr. Bulbul Salwan,** for their unwavering support, wisdom, and belief in me.

This book is also dedicated to the unsung heroes of the OR—the nurses, scrub techs, and perioperative staff who work tirelessly to ensure every surgery is successful.

TABLE OF CONTENTS

TABLE OF CONTENTS

FOREWORD

DR. NATHANIEL SOPER

The operating room (OR) is the epicenter of surgical innovation, where every process impacts patient outcomes and defines the quality of care. Efficiency in this environment is not just operational—it is transformative. Sumit Sharma's book provides a masterful roadmap for optimizing OR operations, marrying practical solutions with a deep understanding of surgical workflows.

With extensive experience in healthcare strategy and a unique perspective from observing over 200 operations, Sumit delivers insights that resonate with surgeons, perioperative teams, and healthcare leaders. His expertise in Lean and Six Sigma methodologies offers proven, data-driven approaches to solving complex OR challenges.

As a pioneer in minimally invasive surgery, I have seen how innovation thrives in well-managed ORs. This book takes a systemic approach to transforming ORs into high-performance spaces where surgical teams can focus on advancing techniques and delivering exceptional care. Sumit's work is essential reading for those committed to driving excellence and innovation in surgical environments.

Nathaniel Soper, MD FACS MAMSE
Professor and Chair, Department of Surgery
University of Arizona College of Medicine - Phoenix

Chair, Department of Surgery
Physician Executive Director, General Surgery Service Line,
Banner – University Medical Center Phoenix

FOREWORD

DR. FARAH HUSAIN

The operating room (OR) is the heart of surgical care, where precision, teamwork, and efficiency come together to ensure patient safety and successful outcomes. Operational inefficiencies in the OR can ripple across surgical programs, impacting care delivery and straining resources. Sumit Sharma's book provides a blueprint for addressing these challenges, empowering surgical teams and healthcare leaders to create more effective perioperative systems.

Based on his firsthand observations of hundreds of surgical operations and deep expertise in process improvement methodologies, Sumit offers actionable and impactful strategies. This book is a resource for anyone seeking to optimize OR operations, reduce delays, and enhance team collaboration.

In my role overseeing surgical quality, I understand how streamlined workflows and coordinated efforts in the OR translate directly into better patient outcomes. Sumit's work equips readers with the tools to make meaningful improvements, ensuring that ORs operate at their best. It is a vital guide for clinicians and administrators dedicated to advancing the standards of surgical care.

Farah Husain, MD, FACS, FASMBS
Ira A. Fulton Endowed Chair of Bariatric Surgery & Metabolic Disorders
Associate Professor and Division Chief of Bariatrics Surgery
Vice Chair of Quality, Department of Surgery
University of Arizona College of Medicine-Phoenix

Surgical Director, Surgery and Metabolic Disorders Service Line
Banner – University Medical Center Phoenix AZ

INTRODUCTION

The operating room (OR) is one of the most critical environments in healthcare. It's where lives are saved, innovation is realized, and teamwork is paramount. However, it is also one of the most complex and challenging areas to manage; requiring seamless coordination between surgeons, anesthesiologists, nurses, perioperative staff, and administrators.

After observing 200+ surgeries in a variety of settings—ranging from inpatient operating rooms to ambulatory and outpatient surgical centers, as well as endoscopy units—I have developed a deep appreciation for the delicate balance between clinical care, operational efficiency, and patient safety. The realization; every element of the OR ecosystem must work in sync to achieve optimal outcomes.

However, the challenges in the OR are immense. Delayed turnover times, scheduling inefficiencies, miscommunication, and resource constraints can lead to increased costs, reduced throughput, and compromised patient care. As healthcare systems grapple with increasing financial pressures, the need for efficient and effective OR management has never been a higher priority.

This book guides healthcare professionals—surgeons, perioperative staff, administrators, and students; seeking practical solutions to optimize OR performance.

Drawing on my experiences as a healthcare leader, process engineer, and strategist; I have combined hands-on insights with proven methodologies like Lean, Six Sigma, and project management to create actionable strategies for improving efficiency, reducing costs, and enhancing patient outcomes.

While this book focuses on operational improvements, its ultimate goal is to inspire a mindset shift—a realization that every improvement, no matter how small, can lead to significant, positive change. Whether you are a surgeon looking to maximize your time with patients, a nurse aiming to streamline workflows, or a student eager to learn about OR dynamics, this book offers the tools and strategies to help you succeed.

Why Now?
The rapid adoption of robotic-assisted surgery, the growing focus on sustainability, and the growing demand for value-based care are reshaping the surgical landscape. As these trends unfold and healthcare delivery becomes more complex, optimizing OR performance is a necessity and a strategic imperative.

This book is not just about solving problems; it is about building resilient, innovative, and patient-centered systems. It is about creating an OR environment where every team member can perform at their best, and every patient can receive the highest standards of care.

A Resource for All
Whether you are a healthcare professional seeking practical solutions, an executive looking for strategic insights, or a student trying to understand the dynamics of the OR, this book is for you. The lessons shared here are not just theoretical—they are grounded in real-world experience and designed for application in diverse settings.

Thank you for embarking on this journey with me. Together, we can reimagine the OR and make a lasting impact on healthcare.

CHAPTER 1

THE FOUNDATIONS OF OR EFFICIENCY
Understanding the core principles of efficiency

Introduction: Why OR Efficiency Matters
The operating room (OR) is often described as the heart of the hospital—a space where precision, teamwork, and resource management are put to the ultimate test. Every minute in the OR holds immense value, not just for the hospital's operations, but also for the patients whose lives depend on timely, effective care. A single delay can ripple through an entire day's schedule, creating staff frustration and patient anxiety.

Imagine a patient named Maria who has waited months for her surgery. As her scheduled time approaches, a last-minute delay occurs due to missing equipment. This seemingly minor issue snowballs, delaying her procedure and the following cases. Staff scramble to regroup while Maria's family grows increasingly anxious in the waiting room. This scene is all too familiar in hospitals worldwide, illustrating how inefficiency in the OR impacts everyone—patients, families, caregivers, staff, and administrators alike.

OR efficiency is about more than just numbers. It directly affects patient care, team morale, and the hospital's financial health marked by rising costs and increasing demand. Addressing inefficiencies is no longer optional; it is a critical step toward delivering high-quality care and maintaining organizational sustainability.

This book explores the principles, challenges, and opportunities that shape OR performance. By examining global scenarios and providing actionable strategies, I guide teams in transforming their ORs into benchmarks of excellence.

With Maria's story in mind, let's examine how OR operations impact not only individuals and the healthcare system, but also staff morale, overall effectiveness, and the long-term sustainability of institutions.

The Role of OR Efficiency in Healthcare

Operating rooms (ORs) are uniquely positioned in healthcare, blending clinical precision with operational complexity. They are not only spaces where life-saving procedures take place, but also significant revenue drivers and cost centers. Achieving optimal OR performance is, therefore, essential for maintaining patient satisfaction and supporting long-term organization viability.

Let's consider the story of a hospital tackling OR deficiencies. On a typical day, the morning begins without issue, but soon a cascade of disruptions unfold. An emergency consultation delays a surgeon, critical equipment is unavailable, and miscommunication leads to duplicate preparation efforts. By day's end, several surgeries are either delayed or canceled, leaving patients disappointed, staff stressed, and the hospital facing financial losses.

This example highlights the duality of OR efficiency. When the OR operates smoothly, it exemplifies healthcare excellence. When inefficiencies creep in, they disrupt the schedule and the hospital's mission to provide timely care.

Revenue Contribution

Operating rooms are a hospital's financial engine. On average, they generate over 60% of hospital revenue, mostly from elective and high-complexity cases. A well-managed OR schedule maximizes revenue opportunities, while inefficiencies result in missed procedures, lost income, and higher costs.

Cost Implications

Conversely, inefficiencies can generate millions of dollars in lost revenue annually due to idle time, delays, or canceled cases. Even a single day of avoidable delays can have a ripple effect, increasing operational expenses and diminishing financial performance.

Impact on Stakeholders

The effects of OR efficiency—or inefficiency—extend far beyond revenue:

- **Patients:** Timely surgeries improve recovery times, reduce complications, and enhance overall satisfaction. For patients, efficiency means receiving care without unnecessary delays or stress.
- **Staff:** Efficient workflows alleviate burnout, increase job satisfaction, and enhance team morale. Staff working in a well-organized OR are better equipped to deliver high-quality care.
- **Administrators:** High-performing ORs optimize financial health and contribute to a hospital's reputation, attracting top talent and building trust within the community.

By focusing on OR efficiency, hospitals can achieve a balance between clinical excellence and operational sustainability. The following section will explore the fundamental concepts that underpin an optimized OR, offering insights into how these elements can transform hospital operations.

Historical Evolution of OR Efficiency

The journey toward OR proficiency reflects the broader evolution of healthcare. Historically, surgical scheduling and resource allocation were manual and often reactive.

The following milestones illustrate how OR practices have developed:

- **Mid-20th Century:** Introduction of standardized surgical checklists, emphasizing safety and consistency.

- **1970s:** Lean methodologies were adopted to streamline workflows in industries from manufacturing to healthcare.

- **1990s:** Emergence of digital scheduling systems, replacing paper-based calendars.

- **2000s:** Widespread use of data-driven tools, including real-time dashboards and predictive analytics.

- **Recent Advances:** Integrating robotic surgery and artificial intelligence to enhance precision and resource management.

These advancements highlight the continuous interplay between technological innovation and operational strategy in improving OR performance.

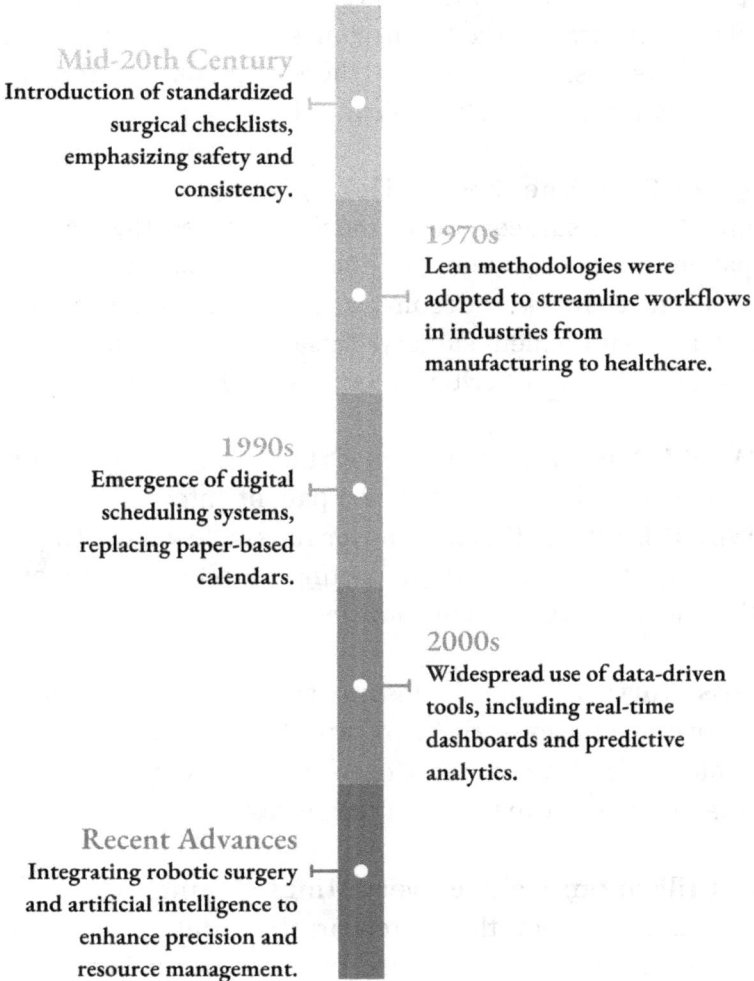

Mid-20th Century
Introduction of standardized
surgical checklists,
emphasizing safety and
consistency.

1970s
Lean methodologies were
adopted to streamline workflows
in industries from
manufacturing to healthcare.

1990s
Emergence of digital
scheduling systems,
replacing paper-based
calendars.

2000s
Widespread use of data-driven
tools, including real-time
dashboards and predictive
analytics.

Recent Advances
Integrating robotic surgery
and artificial intelligence to
enhance precision and
resource management.

Key Components of OR Efficiency

Operating room (OR) efficiency is like a finely choreographed performance where every role, action, and piece of equipment must align to achieve optimal outcomes. Behind the scenes, several key components are pillars of this efficiency. When these elements are seamlessly integrated, the OR becomes a hub of precision, speed, and effectiveness. Let's explore these components through real-world examples and actionable insights.

Turnover Time: The Clock Is Ticking

Picture this: The surgeon places the final sutures, the team wheels the patient out of the room, and the OR team springs into action. Every second counts as the room transforms into a sterile and ready space for the subsequent surgery. This interval, known as turnover time, is one of the most critical metrics for OR efficiency.

- **What It Means:** Turnover time is the duration between one patient exiting the OR and the next patient entering.
- **Why It Matters:** Faster turnover times allow more cases to be completed daily, directly impacting hospital revenue and patient access. But speed must never compromise safety.

Success Story: A California hospital achieved a 12-minute reduction in average turnover times by introducing synchronized cleaning protocols and pre-surgical checklists; thus proving that even minor adjustments can yield significant results.

Block Utilization: Making Every Minute Count

Imagine an orchestra with a set rehearsal schedule. If the conductor or key musicians fail to show up, precious time is lost. Similarly, block utilization measures how efficiently the team applies the allocated time.

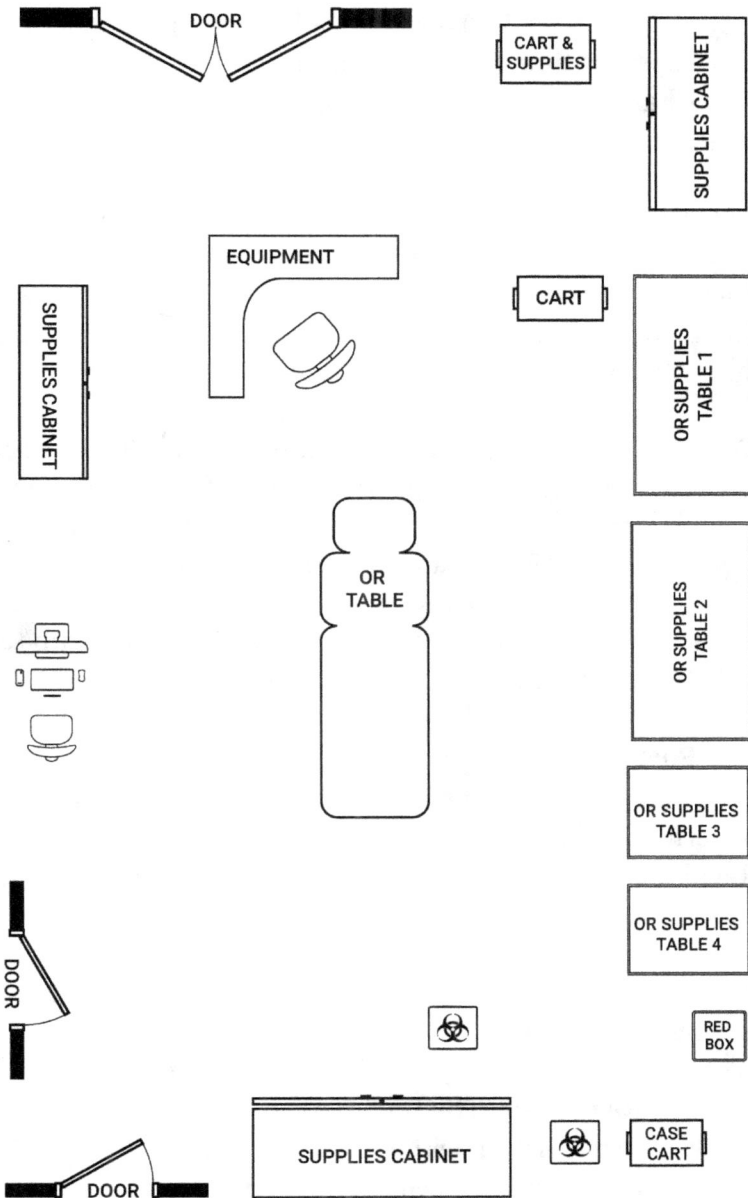

DOOR

CART & SUPPLIES

SUPPLIES CABINET

EQUIPMENT

SUPPLIES CABINET

CART

OR SUPPLIES TABLE 1

OR TABLE

OR SUPPLIES TABLE 2

OR SUPPLIES TABLE 3

OR SUPPLIES TABLE 4

DOOR

RED BOX

SUPPLIES CABINET

CASE CART

DOOR

Purpose: This diagram provides a visual representation of the OR setup and demonstrates the baseline structure needed for efficiency. Placing it here helps introduce the spatial layout for readers.

- **Defining the Metric:** Block utilization is the percentage of allocated surgical time blocks actively utilized for surgeries.
- **The Challenge:** Underutilized blocks lead to idle ORs, lost revenue, and delayed care.

The Solution: Hospitals can harness data-driven scheduling systems to predict surgeon availability and patient demand, ensuring that each block gets filled efficiently. For example, predictive analytics can align high-demand cases with open time slots, maximizing productivity and minimizing waste.

- Collaboration Among OR Teams: The Heartbeat of Success
Collaboration isn't just a buzzword in the OR—it's the lifeline of successful operations. Every team member, from surgeons to environmental services (EVS) staff, ensures smooth workflows.

Key Players: Surgeons, anesthesiologists, nurses, scrub techs, and EVS teams must work harmoniously.

How to Foster Teamwork:
- Pre-surgical briefings bring everyone to the same page, reducing errors and last-minute surprises.
- Regular interdisciplinary meetings create an environment of trust and alignment.

These teams minimize delays and maximize patient outcomes when functioning as a cohesive unit.

Equipment Readiness: The Backbone of OR Productivity
No orchestra can perform without its instruments, and no OR can function without the timely availability of surgical tools. Equipment readiness is a behind-the-scenes hero that often goes unnoticed until something goes wrong.

The Role of CSPD: The Central Sterile Processing Department (CSPD) sterilizes, checks, and prepares every instrument for subsequent use.

The Stakes: Delays in equipment availability are a leading cause of OR idle time, often derailing even the most well-scheduled days.

Improving Readiness: Streamlined CSPD workflows, automated tracking systems, and clear communication channels can significantly reduce equipment-related delays.

Achieving OR optimization is not about addressing one issue in isolation—it's about harmonizing multiple components to create a seamless experience. Whether shaving minutes off turnover times, maximizing block utilization, fostering collaboration, or ensuring equipment readiness, every effort contributes to a larger goal: delivering safe, timely, and effective surgical care.

Challenges in Achieving OR Efficiency

The path to OR optimization is far from simple. Although the benefits—improved patient care, higher staff satisfaction, and stronger financial outcomes—are clear, hospitals frequently encounter substantial challenges. Overcoming these hurdles demands creativity, collaboration, and a readiness to adapt. Let's explore the most common barriers to OR performance and how innovative solutions can transform these challenges into opportunities.

Variability in Surgical Case Types: The Complexity Conundrum
Imagine an OR schedule where a complex cardiac procedure follows a routine knee arthroscopy. The variation in preparation, surgical execution, and recovery times can create ripples that disrupt the day's schedule.

The Challenge: Complex surgeries demand longer preparation times, specialized equipment, and additional recovery room resources, making it harder to maintain predictable workflows.

The Solution: Grouping similar surgeries into dedicated blocks minimizes the need for frequent equipment changes and allows staff to work more efficiently. For example, an orthopedic-focused morning block can reduce setup times and improve overall flow.

Staffing Issues: The Workforce Balancing Act

A well-functioning OR depends on skilled professionals, yet hospitals nationwide face staffing shortages and high turnover rates among key personnel such as nurses, anesthesiologists, and scrub techs.

The Challenge: Staffing gaps can delay surgeries, overburden existing team members, and create inefficiencies throughout the OR schedule.

Success Story: A Midwest hospital implemented a tiered staffing model to tackle this issue. Additional staff were brought in during peak hours to manage demand, while non-peak hours required fewer resources. This approach ensured better coverage without overloading the team.

The Takeaway: Retention strategies such as career development opportunities, competitive pay, and supportive work environments are as critical as addressing staffing needs.

Resistance to Change: Breaking Long-Standing Habits

For many OR teams, established workflows represent comfort and familiarity. Staff often view new efficiency initiatives with skepticism or outright resistance.

The Challenge: Long-standing habits and routines can make adopting new practices difficult, slowing progress and reducing staff buy-in.

The Strategy:
- Engagement: Involve OR staff early in the decision-making process to thoroughly address their concerns.
- Training: Provide hands-on opportunities to learn new tools and techniques, emphasizing change's personal and collective benefits.

When staff members feel like active participants in the transformation, they are more likely to embrace new processes and technologies.

Technological Limitations: Bridging the Resource Gap
Not all hospitals can access cutting-edge tools such as AI-driven scheduling platforms or robotic-assisted surgical systems. Manual processes often dominate in resource-limited settings, leaving little room for error or scalability.

The Challenge: Without access to advanced technologies, hospitals may struggle with inefficiencies that automated tools could otherwise address.

Real-World Example: A rural hospital relied on manual scheduling, leading to frequent overlaps and idle times. By introducing a simple spreadsheet-based system with defined workflows, they reduced scheduling errors by 25% without significant financial investment.

The Insight: Efficiency is achievable even with limited resources as long as hospitals are willing to adapt and innovate within their means.

Turning Challenges into Opportunities

Every obstacle in achieving OR efficiency presents an opportunity for growth and innovation. The key lies in proactive problem-solving and collaboration, whether overcoming variability in surgical case types, addressing staffing shortages, fostering a culture of change, or working within technological constraints. By acknowledging these challenges and developing tailored strategies, hospitals can build a foundation for long-term success. After all, efficiency isn't just about saving time or cutting costs—it's about creating a seamless environment where patients receive the best possible care and staff feel empowered to excel.

Leadership and Culture as Cornerstones

Behind every efficient operating room (OR) is a leadership team that sets the tone and a culture that embraces continuous improvement. Leadership is not just about setting goals; it's about empowering teams, fostering accountability, and building an environment where every member feels invested in the OR's success.

Set Clear Metrics: The Power of Direction

Leaders who establish well-defined goals give teams a target to aim for, creating focus and alignment.

Example: Metrics such as reducing turnover times to under 30 minutes or achieving 90% block utilization provide measurable objectives that drive improvement.

Empower the Team: Flexibility and Growth

A well-trained team is the backbone of OR efficiency.

Actionable Insight: Cross-training staff members ensures that team roles remain fluid, enabling flexibility during high-demand situations.

Celebrate Wins: The Fuel of Motivation

Recognizing success reinforces positive behavior and builds morale.

Simple Gesture, Big Impact: Acknowledging teams for achieving milestones—through a formal award or a simple shout-out during a briefing—can significantly boost motivation.

Leaders who prioritize these strategies cultivate a culture of excellence where efficiency becomes second nature, and every team member feels empowered to contribute to the OR's success.

A Case Study in OR Optimization

Situation: A suburban hospital with six ORs experienced frequent delays and underutilization, with average turnover times exceeding 45 minutes.

Task: Improve OR utilization and reduce turnover times by 20% within six months.

Action:
1. Conducted a time-motion study to identify inefficiencies in cleaning and setup processes.
2. Introduced staggered staffing schedules for EVS teams to ensure continuous availability.
3. Implemented an automated scheduling tool to minimize idle blocks.

Result:
- Reduced turnover times to 32 minutes on average.
- OR utilization increased by 18%, generating $850,000 in additional revenue over a year.
- Staff reported higher satisfaction due to more predictable workflows.

Tools and Technologies Driving OR Efficiency
Innovation is revolutionizing the operating room (OR), turning once-daunting challenges into opportunities for seamless workflows and improved outcomes.

Here's a high-level look at the technologies making a difference:

AI-Based Scheduling Platforms: Smarter Schedules, Smoother Days
Imagine a system that predicts patient flow and staff availability with precision. Tools like Qventus do just that, ensuring every minute of OR time is optimized.

Impact: These platforms minimize scheduling conflicts, helping hospitals maximize their OR capacity while reducing stress on staff.

Real-Time Dashboards: The Command Center of the OR
Use real-time dashboards as the OR's nerve center, providing live updates on surgeries, delays, and resources.

Result: A hospital implementing dashboards saw idle time drop by 15%, demonstrating how instant insights can drive immediate action.

Robotic-Assisted Systems: Precision Meets Innovation
Robotic systems like the da Vinci Surgical System have elevated surgical precision, particularly in minimally invasive procedures.

Outcome: Patients experience fewer complications and shorter recovery times, enabling hospitals to achieve better outcomes while improving efficiency.

These tools enhance OR operations, empower teams to deliver better care faster and more effectively, and set a new standard for what's possible in surgical environments.

Conclusion

OR efficiency begins with a strong foundation of streamlined processes, empowered teams, and informed decision-making. By addressing challenges head-on and embracing innovation, hospitals can significantly enhance patient care, improve team morale, and ensure financial sustainability.

The key to success lies in balancing the art of collaboration with the science of data-driven strategies. As you move through this book, the advanced tools, technologies, and leadership approaches discussed will build on these core principles, offering actionable insights to elevate your OR operations to the next level.

CHAPTER 2

CHALLENGES IN ACHIEVING OR EFFICIENCY
Identifying delays and solving inefficiencies

Introduction

Operating rooms (ORs) are some of the most complex environments in healthcare, demanding flawless coordination of personnel, technology, and procedures. Despite notable progress in tools and strategies, achieving OR performance remains a considerable challenge for many hospitals. Inefficiencies can stem from factors such as resource constraints, miscommunication, and resistance to change, all of which can hinder optimal functioning.

In a multi-hospital health system, facility variations magnify these challenges, leading to inconsistent workflows and deficiencies. For example, differing turnover processes can create significant disparities in OR utilization rates across hospitals, making it critical for system leaders to address these variations through standardization and shared best practices.

This chapter explores hospitals' key challenges in creating efficient ORs, offering a detailed analysis of the underlying causes and their impact on operations. By understanding these barriers, healthcare leaders can create targeted solutions to overcome them.

Staffing Challenges

OR efficiency is a team effort, but it's often stretched thin. The availability, expertise, and adaptability of skilled personnel are critical, yet staffing challenges can create roadblocks that ripple across the entire system. Let's break down these challenges and explore practical solutions.

Workforce Shortages: Struggling to Keep Up

Picture a packed OR schedule overloaded with more surgeries than the staff can manage. This issue goes beyond a logistical problem—it triggers a domino effect, affecting patient care, staff morale, and hospital revenue.

The Impact: Short staffing, especially during peak hours, causes delays and forces team members to take on extra responsibilities.

Real-World Example: A Midwest hospital experienced a 30% rise in surgical cancellations due to a shortage of anesthesiologists, highlighting the far-reaching consequences of workforce gaps.

Solution: Focus on targeted recruitment and scheduling strategies to ensure adequate coverage during high-demand periods.

Turnover and Burnout: A Vicious Cycle

High-stress environments like the OR demand physical and mental resilience, but prolonged pressures often lead to burnout and, ultimately, staff turnover.

The Cause: Long hours, unpredictable schedules, and limited support contribute to dissatisfaction.

The Fix:
- Introduce flexible scheduling to reduce stress and improve work-life balance.
- Wellness programs and peer support systems can provide staff with the emotional tools to thrive in high-pressure roles.

Skill Mismatches: The Hidden Inefficiency

Not every challenge is about having enough people—it's also about having the right skills. A staff member untrained in critical roles during emergencies can slow down processes and increase risks.

The Challenge: Limited cross-training leaves teams unprepared for unexpected demands or sudden role adjustments.

The Approach:
- Cross-training programs empower staff to step into multiple roles, making the workforce more versatile and resilient.
- For example, scrub techs trained in basic nursing tasks can provide additional support during high-demand cases.

Making Staffing a Strength

While staffing challenges may seem insurmountable, targeted strategies can turn this weakness into a strength. Hospitals can build a dynamic and adaptable team that forms the backbone of OR efficiency by addressing shortages, reducing burnout, and enhancing skills. After all, an OR is only as effective as the people who keep it running.

Scheduling Concerns

Scheduling is the heartbeat of OR operations, determining whether the day runs smoothly or descends into chaos. Though often overlooked, poor scheduling can result in inefficiencies, wasted resources, and dissatisfied patients. Tackling these challenges demands both technological innovation and proactive planning.

The Issue with Manual Scheduling

Picture a jigsaw puzzle missing key pieces. That's what outdated, manual scheduling systems feel like—fragmented, error-prone, and unable to adapt to the dynamic demands of an OR.

The Challenge: Manual methods often fail to accommodate last-minute changes, leading to scheduling conflicts and underutilized time slots.

A Smarter Solution: Hospitals transitioning to AI-powered scheduling platforms, such as those that predict surgeon availability and patient flow, report dramatic efficiency improvements.

Block Utilization: Striking the Right Balance

Effective scheduling isn't just about filling slots but optimizing them. Poorly planned blocks can waste valuable time, while overbooked schedules strain staff and resources unnecessarily.

The Underutilization Issue: Empty or poorly utilized blocks can cost hospitals thousands in lost revenue daily.

The Overutilization Issue: Overloading schedules increases the risk of delays and staff fatigue, compromising outcomes and morale.

A Success Story: A regional hospital adopted predictive scheduling tools, which led to a 25% improvement in block utilization. This demonstrates how technology can align resources with demand.

Handling Last-Minute Cancellations

Imagine preparing an OR for surgery only to find the patient isn't coming. Last-minute cancellations disrupt the day's flow, waste resources, and frustrate staff.

The Ripple Effect: Each cancellation represents wasted effort and lost opportunities to serve other patients.

Proactive Measures:
- Strengthen preoperative communication to ensure patients understand instructions and show up on time.
- Introduce financial penalties for no-shows, creating accountability while encouraging better patient compliance.

Transforming Scheduling into a Strength
Effective scheduling is more than just a logistical task—it's a strategic lever influencing every aspect of OR operations. By embracing technology, optimizing block utilization, and proactively addressing cancellations, hospitals can transform scheduling inefficiencies into opportunities for growth and efficiency.

Equipment-Related Barriers
OR efficiency hinges on equipment availability, functionality, and readiness. Delays or malfunctions can ripple through the entire surgical schedule, frustrating staff and patients alike. Addressing these barriers requires a mix of proactive management and strategic investments.

Sterilization and Preparation: The First Step to Readiness
Imagine an OR team ready to start a procedure, only to find critical instruments missing or unsterilized. Such delays are not just frustrating—they're costly.

- **The Challenge:** Delays are frequently caused by inconsistent sterilization processes or incomplete instrument trays from the Central Sterile Processing Department (CSPD).
- **A Real-World Example:** One hospital faced an average 15-minute delay per surgery due to incomplete trays. Multiply this across dozens of cases weekly, and the impact becomes substantial.

- **The Fix:** Automated sterilization tracking systems and stream-lined CSPD workflows can minimize errors and improve instrument readiness.

Equipment Malfunctions: The Silent Disruptor

An OR is only as effective as its tools, but equipment breakdowns can halt operations and force last-minute cancellations.

- **The Impact:** Malfunctioning equipment not only delays procedures but can also jeopardize patient safety.
- **The Solution:**
  Schedule routine maintenance to prevent breakdowns.
  Maintain a reserve inventory of critical tools to ensure re placements are readily available.

Technological Limitations: Outdated ORs in Modern Times

Not all hospitals have the resources to equip their ORs with cutting-edge technology, but the absence of modern tools can hinder efficiency and outcomes.

The Observation: Older ORs often lack advanced tools like robotic systems or real-time data dashboards.

The Strategy:
- Prioritize technology upgrades that align with clinical needs and financial capacity.
- Scalable investments, such as modular robotics or portable imaging systems, offer high impact without overwhelming budgets.

The Path Forward

Equipment-related barriers are not inevitable—they're solvable with process optimization, preventative maintenance, and thoughtful investment. Hospitals can minimize disruptions and maintain seamless surgical workflows by ensuring equipment is always ready and reliable, paving the way for more excellent OR efficiency.

Communication and Collaboration Gaps

Operating rooms (ORs) thrive on teamwork, yet breakdowns in communication and collaboration can derail even the most well-planned surgical schedule. Clear, consistent communication is essential to align interdisciplinary teams and maintain efficiency.

Breakdowns in Interdisciplinary Collaboration: Aligning the Team

Picture a surgeon ready to begin, only to find the anesthesiologist unaware of the schedule. Miscommunication like this leads to unnecessary delays.

- **The Challenge:** Misaligned expectations between surgeons, anesthesiologists, and support staff disrupt workflows.
- **The Solution:** Introduce preoperative huddles to discuss case readiness and post-case debriefings to address issues. These practices foster alignment and create a culture of accountability.

Role Clarity: Who Does What and When?

Ambiguity during critical moments like turnovers can lead to wasted time and errors.

- **The Impact:** Without clearly defined roles, teams risk duplication of efforts or missed steps.
- **The Action Plan:** Standardized checklists outlining responsibilities for each team member ensure smooth transitions and minimize confusion.

Feedback Loops: The Missing Piece

An optimized OR learns from its inefficiencies, but this requires structured feedback.

- **The Problem:** Teams cannot address recurring issues without regular performance reviews or forums for staff input.
- **The Solution:** Establish regular performance reviews and staff feedback sessions to foster continuous improvement and open dialogue.

Resistance to Change

Implementing new processes or technologies in the OR is rarely straightforward. Resistance often stems from deeply ingrained habits, fear of the unknown, or lack of leadership.

Cultural Barriers: Breaking Old Habits

Change can feel disruptive, particularly in high-stakes environments like the OR.

- The Observation: Long-standing habits and fear of failure make teams hesitant to adopt new practices.
- The Strategy: Engage stakeholders early by highlighting how changes improve their day-to-day roles and contribute to better patient outcomes. Transparent communication helps ease the transition.
- Inadequate Training: Bridging the Knowledge Gap

New tools and systems can only succeed if teams know how to use them effectively.

- The Impact: Insufficient training leaves staff frustrated and likely to revert to old methods.
- The Solution: Comprehensive training programs, completed with ongoing support, ensure the smooth adoption of new workflows and technologies.

Leadership Gaps: Guiding the Way Forward

Without strong leadership, even well-designed changes can falter.

- The Challenge: Teams need confident leaders to guide them through transitions and advocate for new initiatives.
- The Approach: Empower OR leaders to champion change, build team trust, and proactively address resistance.

From Resistance to Resilience

By addressing communication gaps and resistance to change, ORs can foster a culture that embraces innovation and collaboration. Through clear communication, comprehensive training, and strong leadership, teams can transform challenges into opportunities for lasting improvement.

The Complexity of Case Mixes

The diversity of procedures performed in an OR adds complexity to scheduling and resource allocation. Each case type has unique requirements, creating challenges that demand thoughtful planning and adaptability. The interplay between routine, high-complexity, and emergency cases often defines the efficiency—or inefficiency—of OR operations.

High-Complexity Cases: The Bottleneck Factor

Complex surgeries such as cardiothoracic or orthopedic procedures often require longer preparation times, specialized tools, and highly skilled teams. These cases are akin to intricate symphonies, with each element needing to be perfectly timed and coordinated.

- **The Impact:** Extended setup and teardown times for these cases can create scheduling bottlenecks, delaying subsequent surgeries.
- **Navigating the Challenge:** Allocating dedicated blocks for high-complexity cases keeps these procedures on track without disrupting the rest of the schedule.

Unpredictable Emergency Cases: The Wild Card

Imagine a day of meticulously planned surgeries suddenly disrupted by an unexpected trauma case. Emergency surgeries are non-negotiable but can throw even the best schedules into chaos.

- **The Strain:** Resources, staff, and OR availability are often stretched thin during emergencies.
- **A Proactive Approach:** Setting aside a dedicated OR for emergencies prevents ripple effects across the day's schedule and minimizes disruptions for elective cases.

Specialized Procedures: The Case for Segmentation

Some procedures, such as robotic-assisted surgeries or laparoscopic operations, require specific equipment and setup processes. Attempting to shuffle these cases across multiple ORs adds unnecessary complexity.

- **The Solution:** Grouping similar procedures in designated ORs streamlines setup, reduces equipment transition times, and allows staff to develop expertise in specific case types.

Example: A hospital that clustered orthopedic surgeries in one OR significantly reduced delays caused by switching out specialized tools.

Measuring the Impact of Inefficiencies

Quantifying inefficiencies is critical for driving change and justifying investments in OR improvements. Inefficiencies affect not just finances but also patient outcomes and staff morale, making it imperative for leaders to understand their full scope.

Economic Consequences: The Hidden Cost of Wasted Time

OR inefficiencies often translate directly into lost revenue. Picture an OR operating at just 60% block utilization while surgery demand grows.

- A Stark Reality: A hospital with a 40% underutilization rate might forfeit up to $2 million annually in potential revenue.
- The Takeaway: Every underutilized block represents a missed opportunity to serve patients and optimize financial performance.

Patient Outcomes: Delays That Hurt

For patients, inefficiencies are more than just inconvenient—they can be life-altering. Delayed surgeries often mean longer hospital stays, a higher risk of complications, and diminished satisfaction.

- **The Human Cost:** Patients waiting for critical surgeries may experience prolonged pain, increased anxiety, and poorer recovery outcomes.
- **The Path Forward:** Efficient OR workflows reduce delays, enhancing clinical outcomes and patient satisfaction.

Staff Retention: The Cost of Burnout

OR inefficiencies do not just affect patients—they also affect the staff who keep the wheels turning. Long hours, avoidable delays, and chaotic schedules contribute to burnout and high turnover among nurses, anesthesiologists, and surgical technicians.

- **The Insight:** Inefficient workflows erode morale, making it harder to retain skilled professionals.
- **A Positive Shift:** Hospitals can foster a more supportive environment by addressing inefficiencies, reducing burnout, and increasing staff loyalty.

Understanding the complexity of case mixes and the far-reaching effects of inefficiencies is crucial for creating meaningful improvements. Hospitals can take targeted actions that benefit patients, staff, and the bottom line, from addressing the challenges of high-complexity cases to quantifying the cost of inefficiencies. By tackling these challenges head-on, OR leaders can transform obstacles into opportunities for lasting success.

Conclusion

The challenges to OR efficiency are interconnected and multifaceted, ranging from staffing shortages and equipment delays to cultural resistance and unpredictable schedules. While daunting, these barriers offer opportunities for innovation and improvement. Addressing them requires an integrated approach that considers their interdependencies, such as how better training and scheduling can enhance teamwork and reduce turnover, ultimately driving efficiency.

This chapter sets the stage for transformation by identifying the root causes of inefficiencies. The following chapters will explore actionable strategies, advanced technologies, and leadership approaches designed to overcome these obstacles. By tackling these challenges head-on, hospitals can elevate patient care, empower staff, and build a foundation for long-term success.

CHAPTER 3

STRATEGIES FOR OPTIMIZING OR TURNOVER TIMES
Improving speed with teamwork and preparation

Introduction

Every minute counts in the high-stakes operating room (OR) environment. Turnover time—the period between one patient leaving the OR and the next being ready for surgery—is a critical measure of efficiency that impacts the day's schedule and the entire healthcare system. For surgeons, it means returning to the work they are passionate about. For perioperative staff, it is a chance to highlight seamless teamwork. For healthcare leaders, turnover time is a tangible opportunity to improve patient care and operational performance.

Far from being just a logistical detail, optimizing turnover times requires innovation, leadership, and a shared commitment to excellence. Imagine the possibilities when an OR functions like a perfectly tuned machine. Where delays are minimal, teams are synchronized, and patients receive timely care. This chapter explores strategies to turn that vision into reality, drawing on practical insights, proven successes, and forward-thinking ideas to inspire healthcare professionals at every level to rethink what is possible in the OR.

Through innovation and collaboration, OR turnovers can become more than a routine task—they can be a hallmark of surgical excellence.

Understanding OR Turnover Time

Turnover time in the OR is more than a simple transition; it is a carefully orchestrated process that requires precision, teamwork, and attention to detail. *The process begins when one patient leaves the OR and ends when the next patient enters.* This seemingly straightforward interval contains critical tasks determining the efficiency and effectiveness of the day's surgical schedule.

Key Components of Turnover

Turnover time isn't just about moving from one case to another; it's about preparing the OR for the following procedure with minimal delays and maximum safety.

Environmental Cleaning: The cleaning crew steps in immediately after a procedure to ensure the OR meets strict sterilization standards. This step is essential for efficiency and infection prevention, a cornerstone of patient safety.

Equipment Setup: OR staff must verify that surgical instruments and supplies are sterilized and meticulously arranged to meet the specific requirements of the following procedure. A missing or malfunctioning tool can derail the entire schedule, making this step one of the most critical in the turnover process.

Patient Preparation: The following patients must be fully prepped, from final consent to anesthesia readiness, ensuring they are physically and mentally prepared for surgery. A well-prepared patient minimizes last-minute delays, keeping the schedule on track.

Why It Matters
Efficient turnover times are the backbone of a high-performing OR.

Here's why they're indispensable:

Increased OR Utilization: Faster turnovers mean more surgeries can be performed in a day, maximizing the value of each OR. Hospitals with optimized turnover times often report a measurable increase in surgical volume and revenue.

Improved Patient Flow: Minimizing delays reduces patient wait times, leading to better experiences and higher satisfaction scores. It's not just about keeping the schedule moving—it's about respecting patients' time and delivering timely care.

Cost Savings: Every minute of idle time translates to wasted resources. By streamlining turnovers, hospitals can reduce unnecessary staff hours, avoid equipment downtime, and significantly cut costs.

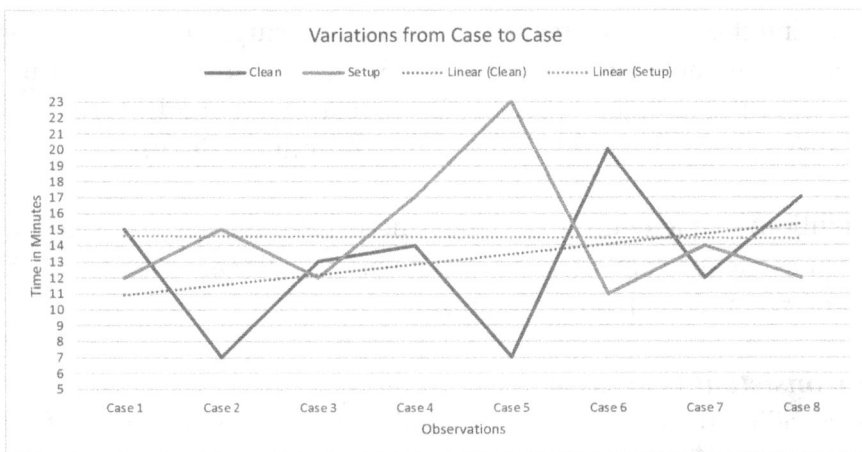

Variations from Case to Case

— Clean — Setup ········ Linear (Clean) ········ Linear (Setup)

Purpose: The graph depicts data-driven insights about cleaning and setup variability, illustrating the need for strategies to reduce inconsistencies in turnover times.

Understanding OR turnover time isn't just about identifying obstacles; it's about recognizing this process's pivotal role in the broader scope of surgical operations. A well-executed turnover ensures operational excellence and enhanced patient care and team satisfaction. In the sections ahead, we'll delve into strategies that transform this critical interval from a potential bottleneck into a benchmark of success.

Current Challenges in Turnover Times

Reducing turnover time is one of the most pressing challenges in operating room (OR) efficiency. It's a complex process involving multiple teams, precise timing, and meticulous coordination. Yet, it is often fraught with barriers that compromise efficiency and create avoidable delays.

Staff Coordination Issues

Effective turnover relies on collaborating seamlessly with environmental services (EVS), nurses, and surgical technicians. However, a lack of synchronization can derail even the best-laid plans.

Imagine this: the EVS team arrives late, the surgical tech still verifies instruments, and the nurse preparing the next patient hasn't received the updated schedule. Each delay compounds, turning a manageable 25-minute turnover into a 40-minute disruption.

Solution: Implementing a standardized communication protocol, such as an automated alert system, ensures all team members are informed and ready to act in unison.

Inconsistent Processes

Variability in cleaning protocols and equipment preparation often results in inefficiencies. One team may meticulously follow a checklist, while another skips steps, leading to confusion and inconsistency.

OR Staff Movement Spaghetti Diagram Analysis

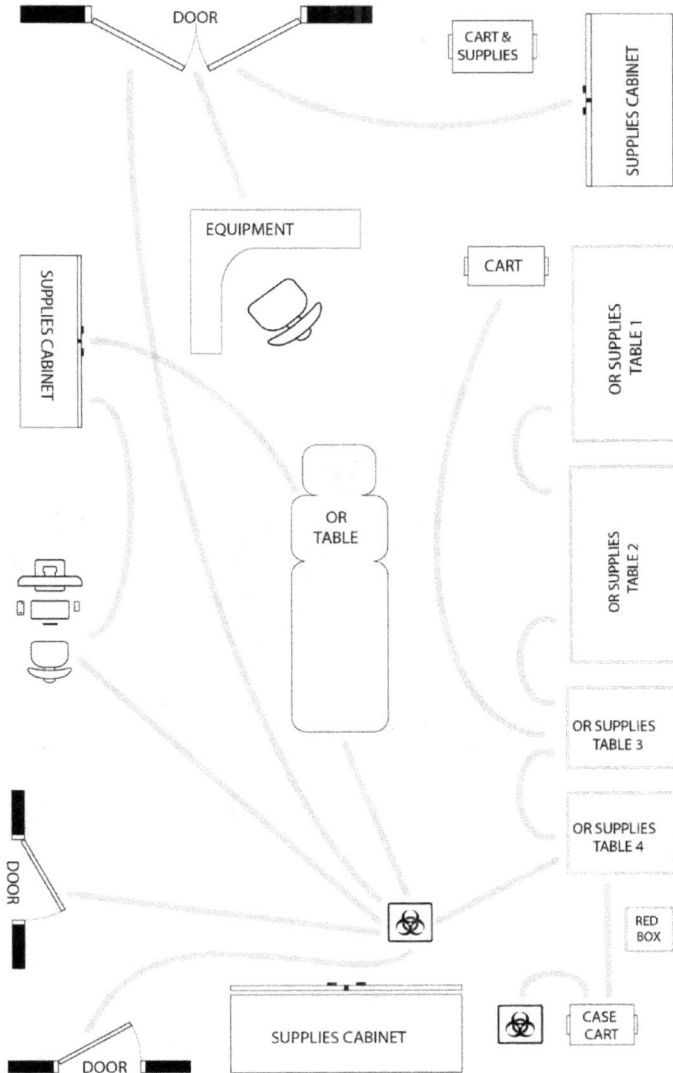

Purpose: These visual highlights inefficiencies related to staff movement and reinforces discussions about inefficient work-flows and coordination gaps.

Example: OR Turnover Time Variability By Case

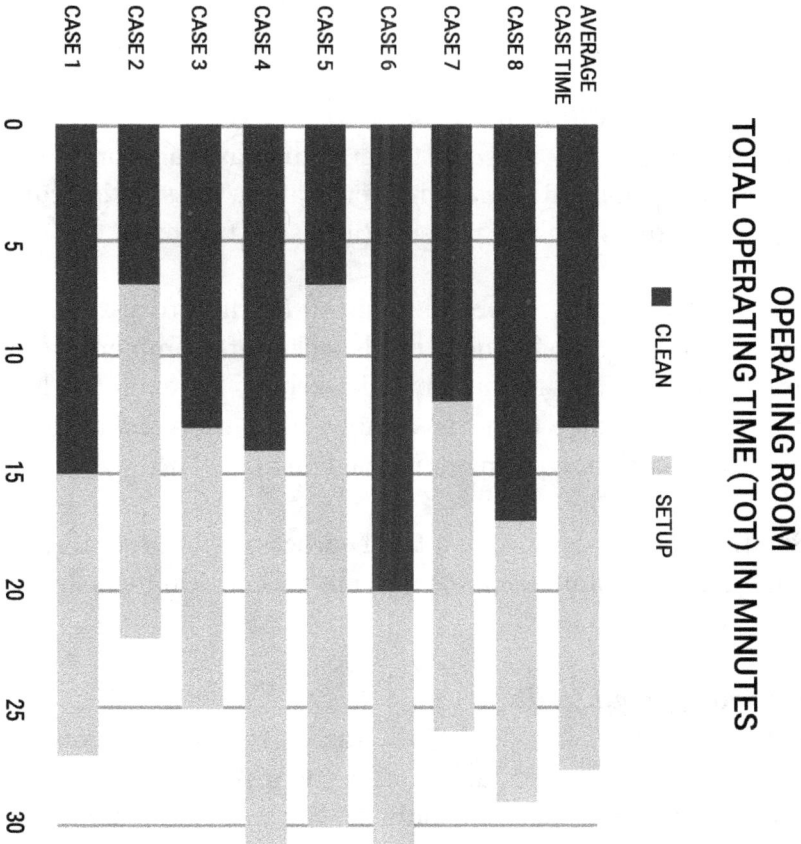

Reinforces Differences Cleanup vs. Setup Durations

For instance, some ORs may prioritize cleaning the room before setting up instruments, while others do both simultaneously. This lack of standardization can lead to redundant efforts or critical oversights.

Solution: Standardized protocols eliminate ambiguity, ensuring that every turnover follows the same efficient steps, regardless of the team on duty.

Equipment Availability

Nothing halts an OR schedule faster than unavailable or improperly prepared equipment. Delays in sterilization, missing instruments, or incorrectly assembled trays can also slow turnovers.

Consider a hospital where the Central Sterile Processing Department (CSPD) faced frequent bottlenecks. After implementing upgraded workflows and automated tracking systems, the hospital reduced its average turnover time by 20%, showcasing the direct impact of efficient equipment management.

Solution: Investing in robust CSPD processes and real-time tracking systems minimizes errors and ensures critical tools are always ready.

Unclear Accountability

In the controlled chaos of the OR, unclear roles and responsibilities can lead to overlooked tasks and bottlenecks. When everyone assumes "someone else will handle it," key steps—like verifying sterilization or preparing the anesthesia station—can slip through the cracks.

Solution: Clearly defined roles and a pre-assigned turnover checklist for each team member establish accountability and streamline the process.

Strategies for Reducing Turnover Times

Optimizing turnover times requires more than speeding up tasks—it demands a holistic approach involving process refinement, technological innovation, and enhanced teamwork. These strategies streamline workflows and foster a culture of efficiency and accountability in the operating room (OR).

Streamlined Cleaning Processes

Efficient cleaning is the foundation of safe and timely turnovers. By leveraging advanced tools and structured workflows, hospitals can save time without compromising safety.

UV-C Sterilization: Hospitals are increasingly adopting UV-C light technology for surface sterilization. This method accelerates the cleaning process and ensures a higher level of infection prevention.

Real-Time Feedback: Checklists and real-time tracking systems help cleaning teams maintain consistency and identify improvement areas, reducing the risk of errors or delays.

Envision a scenario where cleaning teams use handheld devices to check off tasks, instantly alerting supervisors when each step is complete. This transparency fosters accountability and ensures accountability.

Team Coordination Enhancements

Coordination among team members is critical to avoiding delays and redundancies during turnovers.

Pre-Scheduled Roles: Assigning specific responsibilities to each team member before turnover begins eliminates confusion and ensures that tasks progress smoothly.

Time-Motion Studies: Observing and analyzing workflows can uncover hidden inefficiencies.

For example, a hospital identified overlapping tasks among EVS and nursing staff, leading to revised roles and a 15% reduction in turnover time.

Staggered Scheduling

In many ORs, teams perform tasks sequentially, leading to unnecessary idle time. Staggered scheduling allows different teams to work on their responsibilities simultaneously.

For example, While EVS cleans the room, nurses and surgical techs prepare instruments and supplies in parallel, significantly cutting down idle minutes.

Benefit: This approach eliminates wasted time by allowing tasks to run concurrently, streamlining the entire process.

Parallel Room Utilization

One of the most effective strategies involves running surgeries in parallel, especially in multi-room OR setups.

How It Works: As a resident or fellow closes the incision in one room, the attending surgeon can begin the following case in another.

The illustration on the following page 'OR Room Turnover Process Timeline' represents a step-by-step illustration supporting a greater understanding of the specific tasks during room turnover and serves as a guide for identifying bottlenecks.

OR Room Turnover Process Timeline

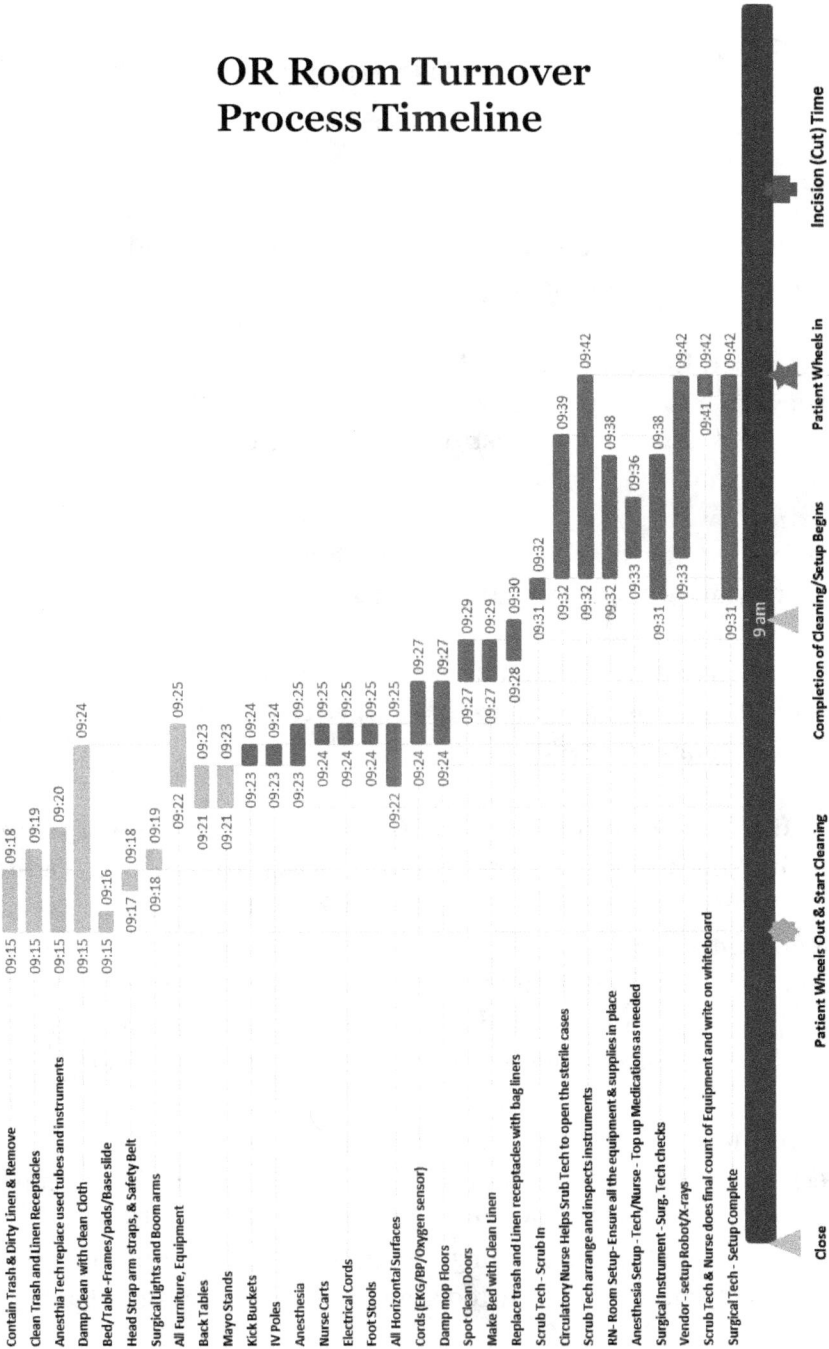

Task	Start	End
Contain Trash & Dirty Linen & Remove	09:15	09:18
Clean Trash and Linen Receptacles	09:15	09:19
Anesthia Tech replace used tubes and instruments	09:15	09:20
Damp Clean with Clean Cloth	09:15	09:24
Bed/Table -Frames/pads/Base slide	09:15	09:16
Head Strap arm straps, & Safety Belt	09:17	09:18
Surgical Lights and Boom arms	09:18	09:19
All Furniture, Equipment	09:22	09:25
Back Tables	09:21	09:23
Mayo Stands	09:21	09:23
Kick Buckets	09:23	09:24
IV Poles	09:23	09:24
Anesthesia	09:23	09:25
Nurse Carts	09:24	09:25
Electrical Cords	09:24	09:25
Foot Stools	09:24	09:25
All Horizontal Surfaces	09:22	09:25
Cords (EKG/BP/Oxygen sensor)	09:24	09:27
Damp mop Floors	09:24	09:27
Spot Clean Doors	09:27	09:29
Make Bed with Clean Linen	09:27	09:29
Replace trash and Linen receptacles with bag liners	09:28	09:30
Scrub Tech - Scrub In	09:31	09:32
Circulatory Nurse Helps Srub Tech to open the sterile cases	09:32	09:39
Scrub Tech arrange and inspects instruments	09:32	09:42
RN- Room Setup- Ensure all the equipment & supplies in place	09:32	09:38
Anesthesia Setup - Tech/Nurse - Top up Medications as needed	09:33	09:36
Surgical Instrument - Surg. Tech checks	09:31	09:38
Vendor - setup Robot/X-rays	09:33	09:42
Scrub Tech & Nurse does final count of Equipment and write on whiteboard	09:41	09:42
Surgical Tech - Setup Complete	09:31	09:42

Milestones: Close — Patient Wheels Out & Start Cleaning — Completion of Cleaning/Setup Begins — Patient Wheels in — Incision (Cut) Time

9 am

Case Study

A large academic hospital implemented staggered workflows across its ORs, reducing the average turnover time by ten (10) minutes and enabling an additional procedure per day.

Enhanced Equipment Readiness

Delays due to equipment issues can derail even the most efficient workflows. Ensuring all instruments are clean, functional, and in place is vital.

Automated Sterilization Systems: These systems streamline instrument cleaning and preparation, reducing manual errors and delays.

Backup Inventory: Maintaining a readily available backup of commonly used tools guarantees that surgeries will not be delayed due to missing or damaged equipment.

Example: A hospital implemented a tiered backup system, storing high-demand instruments closer to the OR, reducing delays by 20%. By integrating these strategies, OR teams can significantly reduce turnover times, creating a ripple effect of efficiency across the surgical schedule. The following sections explore practical tools and case studies demonstrating how staff in various hospital settings can successfully implement these methods.

Technology's Role in Turnover Optimization

Technology has become indispensable in enhancing OR turnover times in today's fast-paced healthcare environment. By providing real-time insights, automating repetitive tasks, and optimizing resource allocation, modern tools empower perioperative teams to achieve unparalleled efficiency.

OR Dashboards: Enhancing Visibility and Coordination
Operating room dashboards offer a bird's-eye view of turnover activities, providing live updates and highlighting bottlenecks in real-time.

Functionality: These systems monitor ongoing turnover tasks, track progress, and alert teams to potential delays.

Example: A regional hospital adopted OR dashboards that synchronized cleaning and setup teams. By alerting staff to their roles and timing, the hospital reduced turnover times by 15% and achieved smoother transitions between cases.

Outcome: Improved communication and accountability across the team, minimizing idle time.

Robotics and Automation: Revolutionizing Turnovers
Automation and robotic systems have emerged as game changers in OR turnover processes, offering speed and precision.

Robotic-Assisted Cleaning: Robotic UV cleaning systems use traditional manual methods to sanitize operating rooms half the time.

Example: A high-volume surgical center introduced robotic cleaning systems, reducing disinfection times by 40% while maintaining rigorous safety standards.

Instrument Readiness: Automated systems ensure surgical trays are sterilized, assembled, and delivered to the OR promptly, minimizing delays caused by manual errors.

Data Analytics: Predicting Needs and Streamlining Resources
Data-driven decision-making optimizes turnover times, particularly in resource allocation and workflow planning.

Predictive Analytics: Predictive tools analyze historical data to forecast peak demand times, allowing hospitals to allocate EVS teams and prepare equipment proactively.

Benefit: During high-demand hours, teams position themselves strategically to ensure seamless transitions.

Example: A teaching hospital used predictive analytics to anticipate staff needs and reduced turnover variability by 20%.

Integration of Systems: A Unified Approach

Technologies work best when integrated into a seamless system. Dashboards, robotics, and analytics tools complement each other to create an ecosystem that drives efficiency.

How It Works: Dashboards provide real-time visibility, robotics handle repetitive tasks, and analytics ensure optimized resources. Together, they enable a synchronized, high-performing turnover process.

By leveraging these technologies, hospitals can transform turnover processes from reactive and error-prone to proactive and precise. The following sections explore real-world applications and strategies for integrating these innovations into established OR workflows.

Case Study: Improving Turnover Time at a Community Hospital

Situation: A 10-OR community hospital's average turnover time was 40 minutes, which significantly impacted its ability to meet surgical demand.

Task: Reduce turnover times by at least 10 minutes within six months.

Action:
1. Introduced a real-time turnover tracking system to monitor progress and identify bottlenecks.
2. Conducted cross-training for EVS and nursing teams to overlap cleaning and setup tasks.
3. Implemented a staggered scheduling model, allowing simultaneous patient preparation and room cleaning.

Result:
- Teams reduced average turnover times by 28 minutes within four months.
- Staff satisfaction improved due to better coordination and more predictable workflows.
- Enabled the hospital to perform 120 additional surgeries annually, increasing revenue by $1.5 million.

Challenges in Sustaining Improvements
Improving OR turnover times is a significant accomplishment, but maintaining these gains presents an ongoing challenge. Sustained efficiency requires constant vigilance, adaptability, and a commitment to continuous improvement. Without these elements, progress can stagnate or even regress, making it essential to address the hurdles that often arise after initial success.

One of the biggest challenges is staff turnover, which disrupts work-flow consistency. New team members, while eager to contribute, may lack familiarity with established processes, causing delays. To combat this, hospitals must invest in regular training and mentor-ship programs. For instance, pairing new hires with experienced team members during their first months can ensure smoother integration and preserve workflow continuity.

Over time, protocol adherence can waver as teams develop short-cuts or revert to old habits. While these deviations may seem minor, they can cumulatively erode earlier efficiency gains. Regular audits, combined with open feedback sessions, help reinforce accountability. These sessions ensure compliance and provide staff with a forum to suggest adjustments that reflect the realities of their day-to-day work.

Even the most advanced tools can lead to technological fatigue if not carefully managed. OR teams may become overly reliant on dashboards or automation, neglecting the problem-solving skills that underpin efficient operations. Leaders must strike a balance by encouraging hands-on engagement and fostering a sense of owner-ship among team members. A culture where staff feel empowered to identify and address inefficiencies can prevent complacency and keep track of improvements.

Practical Tips for OR Teams

Sustaining efficiency is not just about systems and processes but about people. Regular post-case reviews allow teams to reflect on what worked and what did not. For instance, a quick five-minute discussion after each surgery can uncover insights that might go unnoticed. These reviews foster a culture of continuous learning and allow teams to adapt swiftly to challenges.

Celebrating success is another powerful tool. Recognizing high-performing teams or individuals boosts morale and sets a benchmark for others to follow. Simple gestures, such as a shout-out during staff meetings or a feature in internal newsletters, can make a significant difference in maintaining momentum.

Lastly, setting *realistic goals* is key to avoiding burnout. Instead of aiming for dramatic, immediate reductions in turnover time, focus on incremental improvements. For example, targeting a five-minute reduction each quarter provides a manageable pathway to sustained gains while keeping the team motivated and focused.

Conclusion

Optimizing OR turnover times goes far beyond streamlining logistics—it reflects a commitment to operational excellence, patient care, and team collaboration. As explored throughout this chapter, strategies for reducing turnover times range from leveraging advanced technology to fostering a culture of accountability and continuous improvement. By embracing innovation and empowering perioperative teams, hospitals can transform what might seem like an operational detail into a hallmark of their commitment to excellence.

The journey to efficient turnover processes is not without challenges. Sustaining improvements requires vigilance, adaptability, and a focus on technological and human elements. Yet, the rewards—enhanced patient outcomes, increased surgical capacity, cost savings, and higher staff satisfaction—make it an essential focus for healthcare leaders.

In the broader picture, efficient turnover times are a microcosm of what is possible in a high-functioning OR: precision, teamwork, and a relentless drive for improvement. By mastering these processes, perioperative teams and healthcare leaders can set the stage for transformative success in surgical care.

CHAPTER 4

LEVERAGING TECHNOLOGY FOR OR EFFICIENCY
Connecting costs, revenue, and ROI metrics

Introduction

The operating room (OR) often serves as the crown jewel of a hospital's infrastructure—a hub where precision, innovation, and teamwork intersect to save lives and deliver exceptional care. In this dynamic environment, every second matters, and technology has emerged as a game-changer in overcoming challenges and optimizing workflows.

Imagine this scenario: A hospital struggling with frequent delays in surgical schedules due to inefficient room turnover times and miscommunication between teams. After implementing an AI-powered scheduling system and equipping staff with advanced communication tools, the hospital reduced delays and enhanced team coordination. Surgeons could focus more on patient care, and staff morale improved as frustrations caused by bottlenecks diminished. This transformation was about deploying new gadgets and integrating technology thoughtfully to address pain points.

In recent decades, technological advancements have reshaped the possibilities in the operating room. Robotic-assisted surgeries provide unmatched precision, AI-driven analytics predict bottle-necks before they arise, and integrated data platforms keep every team member in sync. These innovations do more than save time or cut costs—they foster an environment where the highest standards of care are consistently delivered.

But with opportunity comes complexity. New technologies require significant investments, training, and cultural shifts. Hospitals must carefully balance the cost of these innovations with the return on investment (ROI) they bring regarding efficiency, patient satis-faction, and financial performance.

This chapter explores the cutting-edge tools and systems that are transforming OR efficiency. From scheduling algorithms that streamline surgical workflows to robotics that boost surgical preci-sion, we examine how these innovations are shaping the future of healthcare. Additionally, we offer practical insights on evaluating, implementing, and scaling these technologies to maximize their po-tential.

By the end of this chapter, readers will understand the impact of technology on OR efficiency and gain actionable strategies to har-ness its power effectively. Whether you are a healthcare leader, a surgeon, or a perioperative team member, the lessons in this chap-ter will equip you to navigate the rapidly evolving landscape of sur-gical innovation.

The Evolution of Technology in the OR

The evolution of OR technology mirrors the broader transformation of healthcare, reflecting the relentless pursuit of better outcomes, efficiency, and patient safety. What was once a simple environment with basic instruments has become a sophisticated space where cutting-edge innovations redefine what is possible. This journey highlights advancements in tools and systems and the evolving mindset surrounding how surgeries are envisioned, planned, and performed.

Early Innovations: Foundations of Modern Surgery

The story of OR technology began in the late 19th century when basic sterilization techniques revolutionized surgical safety. Before the advent of sterile environments, infections were a leading cause of mortality in surgical patients. The introduction of antiseptics, pioneered by figures like Joseph Lister, and sterilization equipment marked a turning point, creating a foundation for modern surgery.

As healthcare advanced, so did the tools. Surgical instruments became more specialized and tailored to specific procedures. From the invention of the scalpel to the creation of retractors and clamps, these tools enabled surgeons to perform increasingly complex operations. Though simple by today's standards, these early innovations represented monumental progress in surgical care.

The Digital Revolution: Transforming OR Workflows

The late 20th century ushered in the digital revolution, transforming how surgeries were planned and managed. Hospitals transitioned from paper-based systems to electronic health records (EHRs), streamlining patient data management and ensuring vital information was accessible to the entire care team. For the first time, surgeons, nurses, and administrators could collaborate seamlessly across a unified platform.

Digital scheduling systems replaced physical calendars, reducing errors and improving coordination. These systems allowed for real-time adjustments, helping to minimize delays and optimize OR utilization. Integrating imaging technologies like MRI and CT scans into pre-operative planning enhanced surgical precision.

The Current Era: Precision and Intelligence

Today, the OR is a hub of innovation, with technology enabling precision and efficiency once thought impossible. Artificial intelligence (AI) and machine learning have become integral to predictive analytics, allowing hospitals to forecast bottlenecks, anticipate resource needs, and streamline workflows. AI-driven platforms help surgeons make data-informed decisions, improving outcomes and reducing variability.

Robotic-assisted surgery, a cornerstone of modern OR technology, allows for minimally invasive procedures with unmatched precision. Systems like the Da Vinci robot enable surgeons to perform complex operations through tiny incisions, reducing recovery times and improving patient comfort. Beyond robotics, real-time data integration ensures that every team member is informed and aligned, creating a synchronized workflow.

Future Prospects: The Next Frontier
Looking ahead, the future of OR technology promises to be as transformative as its past. Augmented reality (AR) and virtual reality (VR) are already making waves in surgical training and planning. Imagine a surgeon practicing a procedure in a virtual OR before stepping into the real one or using AR to visualize a patient's anatomy during surgery.

Autonomous robotic systems, once confined to the realm of science fiction, are on the horizon. These robots could precisely perform repetitive or highly complex tasks, reducing surgeon fatigue and enhancing outcomes. Additionally, advancements in bioinformatics and nanotechnology may enable personalized surgical interventions tailored to a patient's unique needs.

The evolution of OR technology is a testament to humanity's drive to innovate and improve. From the sterile techniques of the 19th century to the AI-driven platforms of today, each step forward has brought us closer to the ideal of efficient, effective, and patient-centered care. As we look to the future, the possibilities are endless, and the OR will undoubtedly remain at the forefront of healthcare innovation.

Key Technologies Enhancing OR Efficiency

Operating rooms are evolving rapidly, with cutting-edge technologies transforming how surgeries are planned, executed, and managed. These innovations are tools and essential components in the quest for greater efficiency, better patient outcomes, and improved team satisfaction. Let us dive deeper into the key technologies reshaping OR workflows and their real-world impact.

Robotic-Assisted Surgery: Precision Redefined

When robotics entered the OR, it marked the dawn of a new era in surgical precision. Systems like the da Vinci Surgical System enable surgeons to perform complex procedures with unmatched accuracy and control. These systems enhance dexterity through robotic arms replicating human movements while eliminating tremors.

Impact:

- Robotic-assisted surgeries reduce hospital stays—on average, 1-2 days shorter than open surgeries—minimizing patient discomfort and speeding up recovery times.
- By reducing complications, robotics also allow surgeons to perform more procedures daily, optimizing OR utilization.

However, robotics comes with challenges. The high upfront costs of these systems and the extensive training required for surgeons and support staff can hinder adoption. Institutions must carefully weigh the long-term benefits against initial investments, often requiring a robust ROI analysis.

AI-Driven Scheduling Platforms: Smarter Resource Allocation

One of the most frustrating inefficiencies in the OR is scheduling conflicts. Artificial intelligence (AI)--powered platforms like Qventus and Epic are changing this landscape by using machine learning algorithms to predict demand, allocate resources, and optimize schedules.

Benefits:
These platforms have been shown to reduce block underutilization by up to 20%, ensuring maximum OR time.
Surgeons benefit from streamlined schedules, which enhance satisfaction and reduce burnout.

Example: A hospital in the Midwest implemented an AI-driven scheduling system and saw an 18% improvement in OR utilization rates within six months. This success highlights the potential of AI to tackle one of the most persistent challenges in surgical operations.

Real-Time Dashboards: Proactive Management

Gone are the days of relying solely on verbal updates to manage OR workflows. Real-time dashboards provide live updates on the status of surgeries, room turnover times, and resource allocation.

Features:
- Dashboards track critical metrics such as block utilization, case progress, and delays, empowering OR managers to address issues as they arise.
- Alerts and visual cues help teams monitor changes, reduce idle time, and ensure smooth transitions between cases.

Outcome: Hospitals leveraging real-time dashboards have reported reduced idle time of up to 15% across their networks, leading to significant time and cost savings.

Advanced Imaging Systems: Elevating Precision
Modern imaging technologies, including 3D imaging and intraoperative navigation, are transforming precision surgeries by offering detailed anatomical views, enhancing accuracy in fields such as orthopedics, neurosurgery, and cardiology.

Impact:
Intraoperative imaging systems reduce the likelihood of errors and enhance surgical outcomes, particularly in high-stakes procedures. They also enable minimally invasive techniques, which lead to shorter recovery times and lower complication rates.

The integration of advanced imaging is a prime example of how technology enhances clinical and operational efficiency in the OR.

Automated Instrument Tracking: Streamlining Preparation
Surgical instruments are the unsung heroes of the OR, and ensuring they are ready, clean, and accounted for is critical. Automated instrument tracking systems using RFID tags are game changers in this domain.

Application: These systems track instruments throughout the sterilization and preparation, reducing human error.

Benefits:
• Missing or unsterilized instruments caused fewer delays.
• Improved compliance with regulatory standards for sterilization.

Hospitals using RFID systems have reported measurable improvements in turnover times and reductions in costly last-minute instrument searches.

Case Study: Transforming OR Efficiency with Technology Situation

Situation: A 12-OR tertiary hospital faced significant delays due to outdated scheduling and equipment management systems.

Task: Modernize the OR with technology to improve turnover times and overall efficiency.

Action:
1. Introduced an AI-powered scheduling platform to optimize surgeon block allocation.
2. Implemented RFID-based instrument tracking to streamline sterilization processes.
3. Upgraded to robotic-assisted systems for high-complexity cases.

Result:
- Turnover times were reduced by 25% within six months.
- OR utilization increased from 70% to 85%.
- Staff satisfaction improved due to reduced manual workload and predictable workflows.

Challenges in Sustaining Improvements
The promise of advanced technology in the operating room (OR) is undeniable, but the implementation journey is fraught with challenges. Hospitals must navigate financial hurdles, resistance to change, and integration complexities to unlock the full potential of these innovations. By proactively addressing these obstacles, healthcare leaders can ensure that their investments lead to meaningful improvements.

High Initial Costs: Balancing Investment and Value

The financial barrier is often the first and most daunting hurdle. Robotic surgical systems, AI-powered platforms, and advanced imaging tools require substantial upfront investments, which can strain hospital budgets. For smaller facilities or underfunded health systems, the cost can feel insurmountable.

The Challenge: High costs deter many hospitals from adopting transformative technologies, even with clear long-term benefits.

Solution: Creative financing options like leasing equipment or forming partnerships with technology vendors can ease the burden. For example, some vendors offer pay-per-use models, enabling hospitals to scale their investment with usage.

Learning Curve: Overcoming Resistance to Change

Even the most innovative technology is only as effective as those using it. Surgeons, nurses, and other OR staff may resist new tools due to unfamiliarity, fear of disrupting established workflows, or skepticism about the benefits.

The Challenge: Resistance to change slows adoption and diminishes the potential impact of technology.

Approach: Comprehensive, hands-on training programs can demystify new systems and build user confidence. Pairing seasoned staff with technology champions—team members who embrace innovation—fosters enthusiasm and accelerates adoption.

Integration Issues: Bridging Old and New

Introducing new systems into an OR is not as simple as flipping a switch. These technologies must integrate seamlessly with existing hospital infrastructure, from electronic health records (EHRs) to scheduling systems.

The Challenge: Compatibility issues can create inefficiencies and limit the effectiveness of new tools.

Strategy: Involve IT teams early in the implementation process to identify and address compatibility concerns. Collaborative planning ensures that new technologies enhance rather than disrupt workflows.

Data Security: Safeguarding Patient Privacy

As hospitals become increasingly dependent on digital systems, the risk of cyberattacks and data breaches grows. Therefore, protecting patient information is crucial for ethical reasons and to comply with legal regulations.

The Challenge: Data breaches can compromise patient trust and expose hospitals to legal and financial repercussions.

Action Plan: Investing in robust encryption, multi-factor authentication, and continuous cybersecurity monitoring can mitigate risks. Regular staff training on data security protocols ensures all personnel are prepared to safeguard sensitive information.

The Path Forward

Although the challenges of adopting OR technology are considerable, they are not insurmountable. Hospitals that tackle these hurdles with careful planning and a flexible approach can overcome them and emerge as leaders in innovation. By proactively addressing financial, operational, and security concerns, healthcare organizations can foster an environment where technology flourishes, staff are supported, and patients receive the highest quality care.

Measuring the Impact of Technology

Adopting cutting-edge technology in the operating room (OR) is only as valuable as the results it delivers. Hospitals must evaluate the outcomes using measurable and actionable data to justify their investments. Beyond the surface-level benefits, tracking the impact of technology provides a clear picture of its effectiveness in enhancing efficiency, improving patient care, and supporting staff.

Imagine a hospital that recently introduced an AI-driven scheduling platform. Initial enthusiasm is high, but how does leadership know if it is genuinely making a difference? Are turnover times improving? Are surgeons and staff noticing a smoother workflow? These questions drive meaningful evaluation and ensure the sustainability of innovation.

Efficiency Metrics: Tracking What Matters Most

Efficiency in the OR is the cornerstone of any technological investment. By focusing on metrics directly impacting operational flow, hospitals can identify what is working and where improvements are needed.

Reduction in turnover times: The decreased time required to prepare an OR between cases indicates smoother workflows and better coordination. For example, a hospital using automated instrument tracking may reduce turnover times by several minutes, resulting in more cases completed per day.

Increase in block utilization rates: Maximizing the percentage of scheduled OR time used for surgeries demonstrates the effectiveness of scheduling and resource allocation technologies.

Financial Impact: Balancing Cost and Value

While advanced technologies often require significant upfront investment, their long-term value lies in the financial benefits they generate. Measuring financial impact ensures that decisions align with organizational goals.

ROI from reduced delays and increased case volumes: For instance, an AI scheduling system might enable the hospital to add one or two additional surgeries per week, translating to substantial annual revenue gains.

Savings from automation: Replacing manual, repetitive tasks with automated systems reduces labor costs and minimizes human error, offering financial and operational benefits.

Patient Outcomes: Enhancing the Core Mission
Every investment in the OR ultimately aims to improve patient care. Metrics related to patient outcomes provide the most compelling evidence of a technology's success.

Decrease in surgical complications and infections: Technologies like advanced imaging systems or robotic-assisted surgery enhance precision, reducing the likelihood of errors and post-operative complications.

Shorter recovery times: Patients benefit directly from innovations like minimally invasive techniques, leading to faster recoveries and higher satisfaction scores.

Staff Satisfaction: Ensuring Adoption and Longevity
Technology is only as effective as the people using it. Engaging staff and evaluating their experience ensures that new systems are integrated seamlessly into existing workflows.

Ease of use and workflow integration: Feedback from surgeons, nurses, and technicians helps identify areas where technology simplifies their roles—or creates new challenges.

Morale and job satisfaction: Streamlined workflows reduce stress and burnout, creating a more positive work environment and improving staff retention.

The Bigger Picture

Tracking the impact of technology is not just about numbers; it is about storytelling through data. For instance, a hospital that reduces turnover times and increases patient satisfaction can demonstrate its commitment to excellence—to its staff and the community it serves. By consistently measuring and sharing these results, leadership can foster a culture of continuous improvement and innovation.

The Future of OR Technology

Tomorrow's OR will become a more dynamic environment where innovation and precision transform surgical care. As emerging technologies reshape healthcare, the potential to enhance OR efficiency and patient outcomes is limitless. The future of OR technology will focus on advancing tools and techniques while creating a seamlessly integrated ecosystem that empowers teams, improves patient safety, and optimizes operations.

Autonomous Robotics: The Next Frontier in Surgery

Imagine a future where fully autonomous robotic systems can perform surgeries with minimal human intervention. This vision might sound like science fiction, but advancements in robotics are rapidly moving us closer to this reality.

The Potential: Autonomous systems could standardize surgical outcomes, reduce variability in complex procedures, and improve overall care quality.

Example: In procedures requiring extreme precision, such as neurosurgery or cardiac interventions, autonomous robots could handle repetitive or delicate tasks with unparalleled accuracy, freeing surgeons to focus on strategic decision-making.

While autonomy may not fully replace human surgeons, the collaboration between robotics and skilled professionals promises a new level of efficiency and consistency.

AR/VR Integration: A New Dimension in Surgery

Augmented reality (AR) and virtual reality (VR) are poised to revolutionize surgical training and intraoperative care. These immersive technologies enhance visualization, helping surgeons plan and execute procedures more confidently.

Applications:
- AR overlays critical information, such as 3D models of a patient's anatomy, directly onto the surgical field during operations.
- VR-based modules offer training simulations for complex procedures, allowing surgeons to practice in a risk-free environment.
- Impact: These tools enhance precision, reduce errors, and accelerate the learning curve for surgical teams, making advanced techniques more accessible to a broader range of professionals.

Smart ORs: The Rise of Intelligent Systems

The concept of a "smart OR" envisions a fully integrated environment where the Internet of Things (IoT) monitors, analyzes, and optimizes every aspect of surgery in real-time.

Features:
- IoT-enabled devices track and manage equipment, patient vitals, and environmental conditions during procedures.
- Automated alerts notify teams of potential issues, such as equipment malfunctions or deviations from expected surgical progress.

Example: A smart OR could automatically adjust lighting and temperature based on the procedure, ensuring optimal conditions for both patient and team while reducing manual distractions.

Predictive Analytics: Harnessing the Power of Data
The future of OR efficiency lies in leveraging data to make smarter decisions. Predictive analytics, powered by artificial intelligence (AI), will enable hospitals to anticipate challenges and allocate resources more effectively.

Applications:
- Historical and real-time data can predict surgical outcomes, helping teams prepare for potential complications.
- Resource allocation tools can optimize staffing and equipment based on case complexity and patient needs.

Example: Predictive tools could identify trends in case delays or turnover times, allowing managers to implement proactive solutions and reduce inefficiencies.

Envisioning Tomorrow's OR
As these innovations converge, the future OR will be more efficient, adaptable, and patient-centered. Hospitals that embrace these advancements will set new standards for care delivery. However, as with any transformation, adopting these technologies will require strategic planning, investment in training, and a commitment to fostering a culture of innovation.

The future of OR technology is not just about the tools but about how they empower teams to deliver safer, faster, and more precise care. By embracing these trends, healthcare leaders can shape an environment where excellence becomes the norm.

Conclusion

Technology is a cornerstone of modern OR efficiency, driving advancements that enhance patient outcomes, streamline workflows, and optimize resource utilization. From the precision of robotic-assisted surgeries to the predictive power of AI-driven platforms, the tools at our disposal have transformed the OR into a hub of innovation and excellence.

However, as this chapter highlights, the successful implementation of these technologies requires more than just investment in equipment. It demands strategic planning, training, and a commitment to integrating these tools seamlessly into existing systems. To unlock the full potential of these technologies, we must proactively address challenges such as high costs, learning curves, and data security concerns.

The future of OR technology is exciting and promising, with autonomous robotics, smart ORs, and AR/VR integration poised to redefine surgical care. By embracing these innovations and measuring their impact through meaningful metrics, healthcare leaders can create ORs that are not only efficient but also adaptable to the ever-changing demands of modern medicine.

As technology continues to evolve, the ultimate goal remains the same: to deliver safer, faster, and more effective patient care while empowering surgical teams and strengthening hospitals' financial health. This chapter underscores that leveraging technology is not just an operational necessity but a critical step toward shaping the future of healthcare.

CHAPTER 5

THE FUTURE OF SURGERY: ROBOTIC-ASSISTED INNOVATIONS AND EFFICIENCY
Maximizing precision and leveraging new technologies

Introduction
The advent of robotic-assisted surgery marks a groundbreaking milestone in the evolution of operating room (OR) practices. Once seen as a futuristic concept, robotic surgery has quickly become a standard of care across various specialties, providing unmatched precision, flexibility, and control. Its potential to improve surgical outcomes while boosting OR performance has made it a key focus for healthcare organizations striving to lead in innovation.

Robotic systems, such as the da Vinci Surgical System and others, are designed to assist surgeons in performing complex procedures through minimally invasive techniques. These systems provide enhanced visualization, magnified 3D imaging, and intuitive instrument control, empowering surgeons to operate with unmatched precision. The implications of these advancements extend far beyond the operating table, influencing patient outcomes, hospital efficiency, and financial performance.

As hospitals and surgical centers increasingly adopt robotic technologies, it becomes essential to understand their operational impact, benefits, and challenges. This chapter delves into the role of robotic-assisted surgery in driving OR efficiency, addressing the practical realities of implementation, and exploring its potential for transforming the future of healthcare delivery.

Key Components of Robotic Surgery

Robotic-assisted surgery has redefined what is possible in the operating room (OR). With technology as its backbone, this transformative approach combines precision, innovation, and adaptability to enhance surgical outcomes. But robotic surgery is more than a collection of machines—it is a carefully orchestrated intersection of technology, human expertise, and operational strategy. Let's dive into the core elements that make robotic surgery revolutionary.

The Heart of Robotic Surgery: Sophisticated Platforms

Consider a system where the surgeon's hand movements directly translate into micro-precise actions deep inside the body. Robotic platforms like the Da Vinci Surgical System have brought this vision to life. With its intuitive controls and multi-arm capabilities, the Da Vinci system allows surgeons to perform delicate procedures with unparalleled precision. From prostate surgeries to complex gynecological cases, it has set the gold standard for minimally invasive surgery.

But innovation does not stop there. The Mako Robotic System, designed for orthopedic procedures like knee replacements, uses advanced imaging to create a personalized surgical plan tailored to each patient. Similarly, platforms like ROSA are making strides in neurosurgery and orthopedics, offering precision that only robotics can achieve.

Emerging technologies are already pushing the envelope. Autonomous and AI-driven systems are in development, hinting at a future where robotic platforms may independently perform routine tasks, reducing the variability of surgical outcomes.

Seeing the Invisible: Enhanced Visualization and Imaging

When performing surgery, seeing every detail matters. Robotic systems provide surgeons with high-definition, magnified 3D views of the surgical field, offering clarity beyond what the human eye can achieve.

Take, for instance, fluorescence imaging—an innovation that allows surgeons to visualize blood flow in real-time. In colorectal surgeries, this capability ensures that resected tissue has an adequate blood supply, reducing complications and improving patient outcomes. These advanced imaging tools are not just technological marvels but game changers that help surgeons make better, faster decisions during procedures.

Ergonomics Meets Precision: Intuitive Controls

Picture a surgeon sitting comfortably at a console, their every movement mirrored by a robotic arm working with microscopic precision. No, this is not science fiction—it is the ergonomic brilliance of modern robotic platforms. The consoles reduce physical strain on surgeons, especially during lengthy procedures, allowing them to maintain focus and accuracy.

Motion scaling further enhances this experience. Robotic arms translate a surgeon's broad hand movements into tiny, precise actions, minimizing the risk of errors and enabling unparalleled control, even in the tightest of spaces.

A Symphony of Instruments

The instruments used in robotic-assisted surgery are masterpieces of engineering. Unlike traditional tools, these instruments are designed to mimic—and often surpass—the flexibility and dexterity of the human wrist. Imagine suturing a blood vessel thinner than a strand of hair. Robotic instruments make such feats possible by performing complex movements and maneuvers challenging even the steadiest human hand.

Take cardiac surgery as an example. Specialized tools like minia-ture scissors and graspers can make precise incisions and manipu-late tissues with micro-movements, reducing trauma and enhanc-ing recovery times.

Integration with a Modern OR Ecosystem

Robotic systems do not operate in isolation; they are part of a broader ecosystem of technologies that harmonize surgical care. These platforms integrate seamlessly with imaging systems like CT or MRI, allowing for real-time adjustments during procedures. Imagine a neurosurgeon mapping the brain's critical regions in re-al-time while the robotic system executes the procedure with pin-point accuracy.

Additionally, robotic platforms are increasingly integrating data an-alytics and predictive tools. These integrations enable innovative scheduling, resource allocation, and even case prioritization, en-suring that every aspect of OR operations aligns with the hospital's efficiency goals.

Preparing the Next Generation of Surgeons

Training is an essential component of robotic surgery's success. Ad-vanced simulation tools provide a safe and realistic environment where surgeons can refine their skills. These simulators replicate real-life scenarios, helping surgeons practice and perfect complex procedures before entering the OR. It is not just the surgeons who benefit. OR staff, including nurses and technicians, receive hands-on training to fully prepare them to support robotic surgeries. This comprehensive approach builds confidence across the entire surgi-cal team, creating a culture of precision and collaboration.

The Patient Perspective

For patients, robotic surgery promises faster recovery and fewer complications. Smaller incisions mean less scarring, reduced pain, and shorter hospital stays. Imagine a patient who once faced a six-week recovery period returning to normal activities in just two weeks—this is the reality for many undergoing robotic-assisted procedures. However, the benefits are not purely physical. Knowing their surgeon is armed with the latest technology gives patients confidence in their care, fostering trust and satisfaction in the healthcare system.

Robotic surgery is replacing traditional methods and redefining what is possible. Robotic systems elevate surgical care by combining cutting-edge technology with human expertise. They empower surgeons to perform with greater precision, enhance patient outcomes, and pave the way for a future

where surgical excellence is the norm, not the exception. As this technology continues to evolve, its role in transforming healthcare will only grow, offering exciting possibilities for providers and patients.

Impact on OR Efficiency

Robotic-assisted surgery has redefined the capabilities of the modern operating room (OR), promising technical advancements and profound impacts on efficiency. This technology shifts the conceptualizing and execution of surgeries, influencing every aspect of the perioperative process. While the road to full integration may involve challenges, the long-term benefits make robotics an indispensable component of the future OR.

Reduction in Surgical Time: Precision with Purpose

Robotic surgery presents an initial learning curve, which can result in longer procedure times as teams familiarize themselves with the new technology. However, as skill levels improve, the resulting efficiencies are striking. For example, robotic systems are known for their exceptional precision. Their capacity to replicate movements with minimal variation significantly lowers the risk of intraoperative complications. This is especially critical in urologic surgeries, where precision is paramount.

Robotic platforms like the Da Vinci Surgical System allow surgeons to perform complex dissections and suturing with unmatched precision, often reducing overall operative time once the team is fully trained. In addition to enhancing accuracy, robotics reduces the need for corrective measures, streamlining intricate procedures. This, in turn, leads to shorter surgical times, quicker turnovers, more efficient schedules, and improved resource utilization.

Streamlined Workflow Coordination

Robotic surgery demands—and fosters—a new level of team synchronization. The preoperative phase benefits from streamlined scheduling and preparation protocols, which ensure the OR is ready when the patient arrives. During procedures, robotic systems create clearly defined roles for team members, reducing ambiguity and improving efficiency. For example, the surgeon operates the robotic console, the assistant ensures instrument readiness, and the scrub nurse monitors procedural needs. Such division of labor enhances coordination, minimizes errors, and reduces unnecessary delays.

Fewer Complications and Reoperations

The precision of robotic systems translates directly into better patient outcomes. Smaller incisions, reduced trauma to surrounding tissues, and minimized blood loss contribute to lower infection rates and faster recoveries. Patients undergoing robotic-assisted procedures often experience shorter hospital stays and require fewer follow-up interventions, significantly alleviating the strain on OR schedules. For example, a comparative study in cardiac surgeries revealed a 20% reduction in complication rates when robotic platforms are employed, underscoring their role in enhancing safety and efficiency.

Optimized Turnover Times

While robotic surgery involves additional setup during initial implementation, its modular design and reusability contribute to long-term turnover efficiencies. Standardized robotic instrument kits and automated cleaning systems allow OR teams to prepare for subsequent cases faster. In high-volume hospitals, robotic systems have demonstrated measurable reductions in turnover times, particularly when integrated with streamlined CSPD workflows and predictive scheduling tools. These efficiencies improve patient flow and reduce idle time for OR staff, creating a more balanced workload.

Increased Case Volume and OR Utilization

Robotic platforms empower hospitals to expand their surgical offerings. By enabling more complex procedures with fewer complications, robotics helps fill OR schedules with higher-value cases. For example, hospitals that adopt robotics often see increased patient referrals for advanced procedures like robotic-assisted oncologic surgeries. This boosts the hospital's reputation and optimizes OR utilization rates, making every resource—from personnel to equipment—work harder and smarter.

Elevated Surgeon Efficiency and Well-Being

A less obvious but critical benefit of robotics is its impact on the surgeons themselves. Traditional surgeries can strain surgeons physically, particularly during lengthy or complex cases. Robotic consoles, designed with ergonomics in mind, minimize fatigue and repetitive strain injuries. This occurrence is not just about comfort—it is about longevity. Surgeons who experience less physical strain can perform more cases over their careers, contributing to overall OR efficiency and continuity of care.

Scalability Across Systems

Robotic platforms are highly adaptable, making them ideal for scaling across healthcare systems. Hospitals can create consistent robotic surgery programs that benefit multiple facilities with proper training and leadership commitment. Hospitals with established training programs report higher utilization rates across their robotic systems as staff confidence and expertise grow. This scalability ensures that the investment in robotics yields systemwide benefits, from better outcomes to increased procedural volume.

Robotics as a Catalyst for OR Efficiency

Robotic-assisted surgery is more than a technological marvel—it is a strategic asset that redefines what is possible in the OR. Robotics transforms efficiency at every level by improving precision, reducing complications, and streamlining workflows. With the proper training, planning, and leadership support, hospitals can harness the full potential of this innovation, turning challenges into opportunities and making the OR a hub of excellence.

Challenges and Considerations

While robotic surgery's promise is compelling, the journey to implementation and sustainability is not without hurdles. Recognizing and addressing these challenges is crucial for realizing robotics' full potential in the OR.

High Initial Costs

The financial investment required for robotic platforms is substantial. A single system can cost between $1 million and $2.5 million, not including annual maintenance and consumable expenses. Hospitals often face pressure to justify these costs. High case volumes and efficient scheduling are key to achieving a return on investment (ROI). Innovative financing models, such as leasing or vendor partnerships, can mitigate upfront financial burdens and make robotics more accessible.

Learning Curve and Training

The transition to robotic surgery requires significant time and resources for training. Surgeons, nurses, and technicians must achieve proficiency in operating the systems and adapting to the new workflows robotics introduces. Training simulators, while valuable, add to the overall cost. However, hospitals that invest in robust training programs often see faster adoption and higher utilization rates, offsetting these initial expenditures.

Integration with Existing Workflows

Adopting robotic systems can disrupt established processes. Scheduling robotic cases, managing equipment, and coordinating teams require adjustments that can initially slow down OR operations.

Hospitals should pilot robotic programs in select ORs before expanding to address this, ensuring workflow and staff are acclimated. Regular feedback loops between robotic teams and administrators help refine these processes.

Access and Equity

Not all hospitals can afford robotic platforms, especially those in rural or low-resource settings. This disparity limits access to advanced surgical care for many patients. Addressing this requires systemic solutions, such as government grants or shared-use models, where smaller facilities partner with larger hospitals to access robotic systems.

Turning Challenges into Opportunities

The obstacles to robotic surgery are real but surmountable with strategic planning, strong leadership, and collaborative effort. By addressing these challenges head-on, hospitals can position robotics as a tool for innovation and a cornerstone of modern surgical efficiency.

Case Study: Transforming Efficiency with Robotic-Assisted Surgery

Background: A mid-sized urban hospital sought to improve its OR efficiency while expanding its surgical service offerings. Leadership identified robotic-assisted surgery as a strategic opportunity to attract high-acuity cases, enhance patient outcomes, and reduce turnover times. However, the hospital faced challenges, including high initial costs, a steep learning curve for staff, and resistance to adopting new workflows.

Implementation
The hospital began its robotic program with the purchase of a state-of-the-art robotic system, accompanied by a comprehensive implementation plan:

1. **Training and Education:**
- Surgeons and OR staff participated in vendor-provided training programs, including simulator practice and live-case mentorship.
- A dedicated robotic coordinator was appointed to oversee scheduling, equipment management, and staff readiness.

2. **Process Redesign:**
- Turnover workflows were optimized by introducing standardized robotic setup protocols.
- Preference cards for robotic cases were updated to ensure consistent instrument availability.

3. **Data-Driven Strategy:**
- Leadership utilized real-time dashboards to monitor OR metrics, including robotic case volume, turnover times, and procedural outcomes.

- Monthly reviews of performance data guided continuous improvement efforts.

Outcomes

After one year, the hospital achieved significant improvements:
- Increased Case Volume: Robotic case volume rose by 35%, driven by the hospital's ability to attract complex surgical cases.
- Reduced Turnover Times: Standardized protocols shaved 8 minutes off average turnover times for robotic cases, resulting in an additional 2–3 cases per week.

Improved Patient Outcomes:
- Compared to traditional laparoscopic surgeries, post-operative complication rates decreased by 20% for robotic cases.
- Patient satisfaction scores improved due to faster recovery times and reduced surgical trauma.

Financial Gains:
- The hospital generated an additional $3 million in revenue from increased case volume and higher acuity procedures.
- ROI for the robotic system was achieved within 18 months, ahead of the projected 24-month timeline.

Lessons Learned
- *Invest in Training:* Comprehensive training programs were critical to overcoming the learning curve and resistance from staff.
- *Standardize Workflows:* Clear protocols minimized variability and reduced setup times, ensuring smooth integration of robotic cases into the OR schedule.
- *Leverage Data:* Real-time analytics provided actionable insights, enabling the team to refine processes and improve efficiency continuously.

Conclusion

This case study highlights the transformative potential of robotic-assisted surgery when supported by effective leadership, strategic planning, and robust operational frameworks. While challenges remain, the hospital's success demonstrates how thoughtful implementation can maximize the benefits of robotic technology, enhancing both efficiency and patient care.

Future Trends in Robotic Surgery

As robotic-assisted surgery continues to evolve, new technologies and methodologies are reshaping its role in the operating room (OR). These trends promise to enhance precision, reduce costs, and expand access to advanced surgical care, driving the next wave of innovation in healthcare.

Artificial Intelligence (AI) Integration: Smarter Surgery

Artificial intelligence (AI) integration is revolutionizing robotic surgery, adding a layer of intelligence to already sophisticated systems.

Predictive Analytics: AI algorithms analyze patient data preoperatively to identify potential risks and optimize surgical plans. By integrating these analytics, surgeons can anticipate complications and make more informed decisions.

- Example: In colorectal surgeries, AI-driven robots have shown promise in detecting small polyps often missed during manual procedures.

Real-Time Decision Support: Advanced AI systems provide intraoperative guidance, such as suggesting the optimal path for incisions or flagging abnormalities during the procedure.

- Example: In tumor resections, AI-equipped robots can distinguish between healthy and cancerous tissue, significantly improving precision and outcomes.

Miniaturized and Portable Robots: Expanding Accessibility

The future of robotic surgery features compact, portable systems that are revolutionizing the location and methods of performing procedures.

Compact Systems for Ambulatory Settings: These smaller robots are ideal for outpatient clinics and ambulatory surgery centers, bringing advanced care to less intensive settings.

- Example: Miniature robotic devices are being tested for gastrointestinal endoscopy to conduct diagnostic procedures and perform minor interventions with minimal invasiveness.

Affordability and Usability: Smaller and simpler systems reduce both the financial and logistical barriers to adoption, making robotic surgery more accessible to rural and resource-limited facilities.

Autonomous Surgical Robots: The Next Leap

While still in development, autonomous robots could revolutionize surgery by performing routine tasks without constant human oversight.

Capabilities: These systems are designed to perform specific tasks, such as suturing or drilling, with remarkable precision.

Potential: Autonomous robots can fill gaps in surgeon availability, particularly in underserved regions.

Ethical Considerations: Their use raises questions about liability and decision-making in complex surgical scenarios that the technology must address as it matures.

Cost-Effective Innovations: Breaking Financial Barriers

Manufacturers are actively working to reduce the financial burden of robotic systems, making them more accessible to a wider range of healthcare providers.

Reusable Instruments: Introducing reusable components significantly lowers per-case costs and enhances affordability.

Subscription Models: Pay-per-use or leasing models offer smaller hospitals the opportunity to adopt robotic surgery without the burden of high upfront costs.

- Example: A small regional hospital successfully implemented a robotic system through a subscription model, performing 150 surgeries in its first year with minimal financial strain.

Tele-Robotics and Remote Surgery: Surgery Without Borders
Tele-robotics are poised to redefine accessibility, enabling expert surgeons to operate from almost anywhere in the world.

Applications: These systems are invaluable in rural or underserved areas where specialist surgeons are unavailable.

- Example: A telerobotic surgery was performed across continents, connecting a surgeon in the U.S. with a patient in Europe, demonstrating the potential of global surgical collaboration.

Challenges: Dependence on high-speed internet and robust cybersecurity measures remain critical barriers to widespread adoption.

Personalized Surgery: Tailored Precision
The future of robotic surgery focuses on personalization, tailoring procedures to each patient's unique anatomy and needs.

Pre-Surgical Planning: Advanced imaging and 3D modeling allow robotic systems to execute patient-specific surgical plans with extraordinary precision.

- Example: In orthopedic surgeries, preoperative models ensure implants fit perfectly, reducing complications and recovery time.

Improved Outcomes: Personalized approaches minimize risks, optimize surgical performance, and enhance patient recovery trajectories.

Collaborative Robotics: Enhancing Team Efficiency

Collaborative robots, or "co-bots," are designed to work alongside human teams, complementing their skills rather than replacing them.

Applications: Co-bots assist with tasks such as holding instruments, retracting tissue, or delivering supplies during surgery, reducing physical strain on human staff.

- Example: In spinal surgeries, co-bots hold retractors in place, allowing surgeons to focus on complex maneuvers.

Benefits: These robots boost efficiency by allowing the surgical team to concentrate on more intricate tasks, improving workflow and outcomes.

Environmental Sustainability: A Greener Future

The growing adoption of robotic surgery also demands a focus on minimizing environmental impact.

Eco-Friendly Designs: Manufacturers are developing systems with sustainable materials and energy-efficient operations.

- Example: A robotic system with recyclable components reduced waste by 30% in a high-volume hospital.

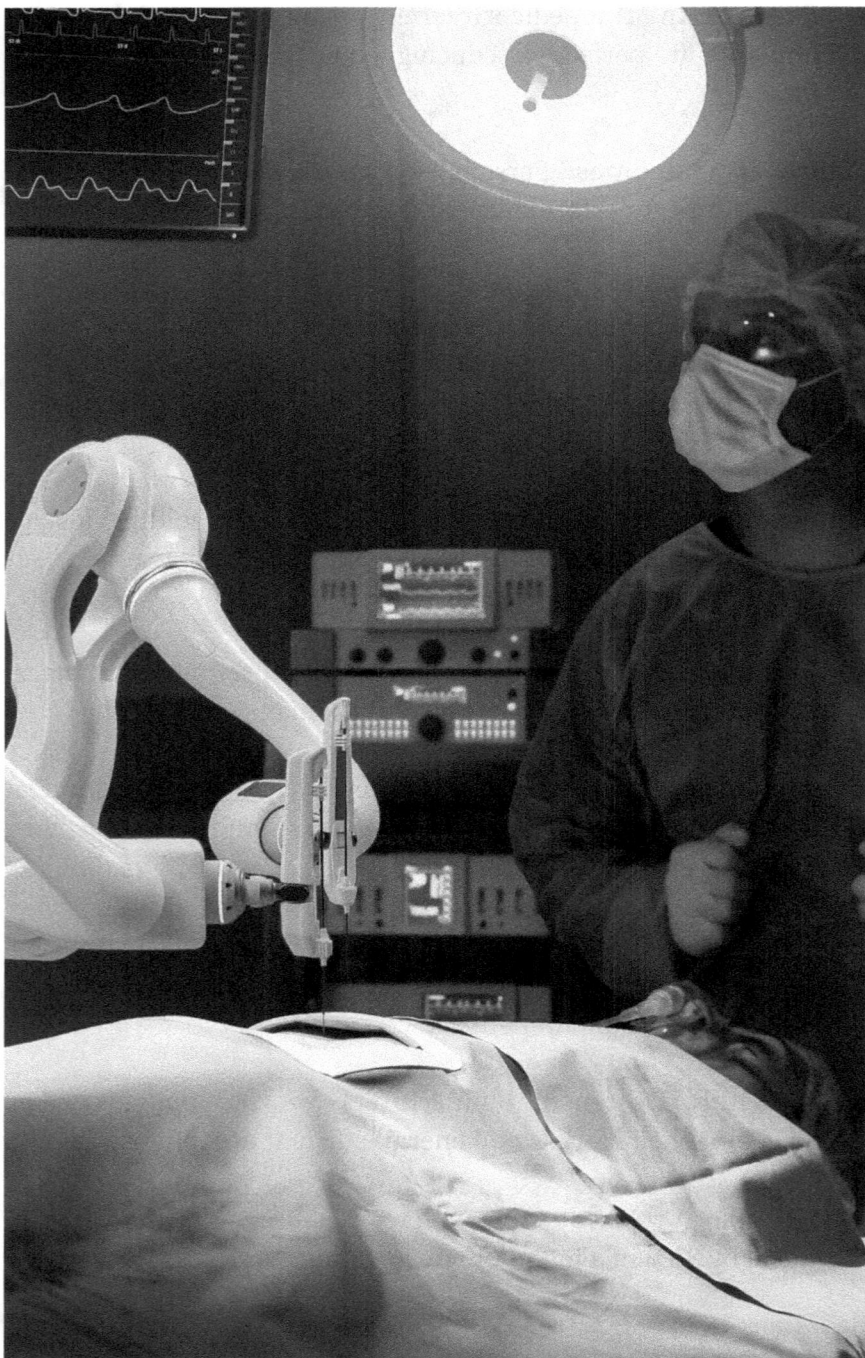

Reducing Disposable Waste: Efforts to create reusable or biodegradable surgical instruments are gaining momentum, addressing concerns about medical waste.

Conclusion
Robotics at the Forefront of Surgical Evolution
Robotic-assisted surgery stands as a beacon of innovation in the modern operating room, redefining what is possible in terms of precision, efficiency, and patient outcomes. While its adoption comes with financial, operational, and cultural challenges, its potential to transform surgical care is undeniable.

As healthcare leaders and professionals, the focus must always remain on leveraging these advancements responsibly. It is critical to balance the promise of technology with pragmatic considerations, such as cost-effectiveness, training, and equitable access. By integrating robotic systems thoughtfully into OR operations, organizations can unlock new opportunities to serve patients better, attract top-tier talent, and achieve financial sustainability.

Leadership plays a pivotal role in this journey. Setting a clear vision, empowering teams, and fostering a culture of continuous improvement ensures the long-term success of robotic programs. Integrating data-driven strategies, standardized workflows, and cross-disciplinary collaboration will further amplify the impact of robotic systems.

Ultimately, robotic-assisted surgery adds value not only through the technology itself, but through its implementation to improve patient care. Every decision should answer the core question: **How does this help the patient?** By maintaining this focus, robotic surgery will continue to serve its higher purpose—transforming lives through innovation and excellence.

CHAPTER 6

ENHANCING COLLABORATION IN THE OPERATING ROOM
Teamwork, communication, and efficiency

Introduction

The operating room (OR) is a high-stakes environment where precision, timing, and coordination are essential. Amidst the hum of machinery and the focused efforts of surgeons, anesthesiologists, nurses, and technicians, collaboration forms the backbone of every successful procedure. However, the OR is not immune to miscommunication, role ambiguity, and interpersonal conflicts, which can jeopardize patient safety and operational efficiency.

True collaboration in the OR goes beyond individual expertise—it is about fostering an environment where every team member feels empowered to contribute, share insights, and work toward a common goal. The stakes are high: seamless teamwork saves lives, reduces delays, minimizes errors, and enhances staff morale.

This chapter will explore the strategies and tools that elevate collaboration from a routine practice to an integral component of surgical excellence. Through real-world examples, innovative solutions, and actionable insights, this chapter will highlight how fostering a culture of collaboration can transform the OR into a well-orchestrated symphony of teamwork and efficiency.

The Importance of Collaboration in OR Efficiency
In the operating room (OR), collaboration is more than a buzzword—it is a necessity. The success of any surgical procedure relies on a seamless interplay between surgeons, anesthesiologists, nurses, and technicians. Each team member's contribution is critical, and when collaboration falters, the repercussions can ripple across patient safety, operational efficiency, and staff morale.

Improved Patient Safety Through Collaboration
In the OR, safety is paramount, and communication is its cornerstone. A surgical procedure involves numerous moving parts, each requiring precise coordination to minimize errors. Effective communication ensures all team members are aligned and equipped to anticipate potential challenges during preoperative briefings or intraoperative updates.

For example, a 2019 study revealed that surgical teams conducting structured preoperative briefings experienced a 50% reduction in errors compared to teams that skipped this step. These briefings allow teams to address patient-specific considerations, review the surgical plan, and clarify roles, creating an environment where everyone is prepared and confident.

Operational Efficiency as a Collaborative Outcome
Collaboration directly impacts the OR's efficiency. Disorganized workflows, unclear responsibilities, or communication gaps can lead to delays disrupting the surgical schedule. In contrast, a well-coordinated team operates like a finely tuned machine, reducing turnover times and optimizing the use of resources. For instance, hospitals with structured interdisciplinary collaboration have reported up to a 15% reduction in turnover times. This improvement translates to more cases completed daily, less downtime, and a smoother overall schedule, benefiting patients and healthcare providers.

Boosting Staff Satisfaction Through Teamwork

Collaboration is pivotal to staff well-being by preventing burnout in the high-pressure OR environment. Strained team dynamics can contribute to burnout, highlighting the importance of effective teamwork. Clear communication and mutual respect, however, foster a sense of trust and camaraderie, creating a supportive atmosphere even during challenging procedures.

Teams that communicate effectively report higher job satisfaction and lower turnover rates. When staff feel heard, valued, and supported, they are more engaged in their work, which ultimately translates to better patient care and a more cohesive OR environment.

Barriers to Collaboration in the OR

Despite its importance, achieving true collaboration in the OR is challenging. The dynamics of surgical teams often include hierarchical structures, cultural differences, and high stress levels, all of which can hinder effective teamwork.

Overcoming Hierarchical Structures

Traditional hierarchies in the OR can discourage open communication, especially from junior team members. This dynamic can lead to missed opportunities for early problem identification or innovative solutions. Encouraging a flat hierarchy during procedures—where everyone, regardless of rank, feels empowered to voice concerns—can significantly improve team performance.

Clarifying Roles to Avoid Ambiguity

Ambiguity in roles and responsibilities is one of the most common pitfalls in the operating room (OR). Confusion can quickly arise when multiple team members perform overlapping duties in a high-stakes environment. When roles are unclear, team members may duplicate or neglect critical tasks, resulting in delays, errors, or compromised patient safety. Proactively addressing this challenge

The Consequences of Role Ambiguity

When team members are unsure of their responsibilities, inefficiencies ripple through the surgical process.

For instance:

- Delays in Turnover Times: If no one is assigned to prepare the surgical instruments while another team cleans the room, the process wastes valuable time.
- Errors in Task Execution: Two nurses preparing the same equipment while other critical tasks remain unfinished can confuse and elevate the risk of errors.
- Increased Stress: Unclear roles foster tension among team members, as individuals may feel overburdened or uncertain about their contributions. This situation can escalate into frustration and miscommunication during critical moments.

Strategies to Define and Clarify Roles

Preoperative Role Assignments

- Conduct a preoperative briefing to explicitly identify roles and responsibilities for the entire team.
- Use a standardized checklist that assigns specific tasks to each team member, from environmental cleaning to instrument setup and patient preparation.
- Example: At a teaching hospital, determining preoperative role assignments reduced turnover times by 12% and improved staff satisfaction, as every team member knew the expectations.

Task-Specific Protocols

- Develop detailed protocols for recurring tasks, such as who is responsible for preparing the anesthesia machine or ensuring all surgical instruments are sterilized and present.
- Example: A hospital created laminated cards outlining the roles of scrub techs, circulating nurses, and anesthesiologists during each phase of surgery, which significantly reduced miscommunication.

Role Redundancy for High-Risk Situations
- Assign backup roles for critical tasks to ensure continuity in case of unexpected delays or emergencies, preventing any essential activities from being overlooked.
- Example: While one nurse preps the patient, another reviews the checklist to ensure all required consents are signed and available.

Cross-Training for Flexibility
- Encourage cross-training among staff so team members can step into different roles when necessary, ensuring a seamless workflow.
- Benefit: Cross-trained teams can adapt quickly to emergencies or staffing shortages, reducing the risk of delays caused by unforeseen circumstances.

Use of Visual Aids
- Implement visual tools, such as whiteboards or digital dashboards, that display assigned roles and their completion status in real-time.
- Example: A surgical center introduced a dashboard visible to the OR team, listing tasks and their assignees. This tool improved accountability and reduced redundant efforts.

Benefits of Clear Role Assignments
- *Improved Efficiency:* Clear roles ensure tasks are completed in parallel rather than sequentially, reducing bottlenecks and maximizing time utilization.
- *Enhanced Patient Safety:* Defined responsibilities leave less room for errors or omissions, especially during critical phases such as anesthesia administration or instrument sterilization.
- *Stronger Team Dynamics:* When everyone knows their role, the OR operates like a well-oiled machine, fostering mutual respect and reducing conflict.

Navigating Conflict and Miscommunication

The high-stress environment of the OR can exacerbate tensions, leading to conflicts among team members. Addressing these conflicts proactively through conflict resolution training and fostering a culture of mutual respect ensures smoother interactions and better outcomes.

Standardizing Communication Across Diverse Teams

Cultural and language differences can create barriers to effective communication. Implementing standardized protocols, such as checklists or the SBAR (Situation, Background, Assessment, Recommendation) communication framework, ensures clarity and consistency, even in diverse teams. By addressing these barriers and implementing intentional strategies, hospitals can create OR environments where collaboration thrives, enhancing patient outcomes and staff satisfaction. In the following sections, we will explore practical tools and innovative approaches to strengthening cooperation and building a culture of teamwork in the OR.

Case Study: Building a Collaborative OR Culture

Situation: A large urban hospital struggled with frequent miscommunications and staff dissatisfaction, resulting in high turnover times and increased procedural errors.

Task: Foster a culture of collaboration to improve OR efficiency and staff morale.

Action:
1. Introduced preoperative briefings and post-operative debriefings for all surgical cases.
2. Conducted quarterly team-building workshops to improve interpersonal relationships.
3. Implemented real-time communication tools to streamline information sharing.

Result:
- Procedural errors were reduced by 25% within a year.
- Staff satisfaction scores increased by 40%.
- Average turnover times decreased by 10 minutes per case.

Measuring Collaboration's Impact
Collaboration in the operating room (OR) is not a one-time achievement but a continuous effort that requires careful evaluation and reinforcement. By measuring key indicators and fostering a culture of teamwork, hospitals can ensure that collaboration becomes a cornerstone of OR efficiency and patient care. This section explores how to assess the impact of collaboration strategies and sustain them for long-term success.

Measuring Collaboration's Impact: Metrics That Matter

Quantifying the effectiveness of collaboration is essential for identifying areas of improvement and demonstrating tangible benefits. Hospitals can rely on specific metrics to track progress and validate the importance of teamwork in the OR.

Procedural Accuracy

Collaboration directly influences the precision of surgical procedures, reducing the likelihood of errors that can jeopardize patient safety.

- Metric: Reduction in errors during surgeries.
- Example: A study revealed that teams engaging in preoperative briefings experienced a 50% decrease in adverse events, highlighting the value of aligned communication.

Turnover Times

Smooth transitions between surgeries depend on coordinated efforts from the entire OR team.

- Metric: Reduction in delays between surgeries.
- Benefit: Improved collaboration accelerates turnovers, allowing for more efficient OR time use.
- Example: Hospitals prioritizing teamwork during turnovers have reported up to 15% time savings, enabling additional surgery daily in high-volume centers.

Staff Satisfaction

A collaborative environment fosters positive relationships, reduces stress, and boosts morale among OR staff.

- Metric: Post-surgery surveys and retention rates.
- Example: Facilities with robust collaboration protocols report a 30% lower turnover rate among OR staff, reflecting a happier and more cohesive workforce.

Patient Outcomes

Effective collaboration leads to improved patient experiences and better clinical results.

- Metric: Reduced complication rates and improved recovery times.
- Impact: Teams that communicate effectively deliver timely and precise care, minimizing post-operative complications and enhancing patient satisfaction.

Sustaining a Collaborative Culture: Strategies for Long-Term Success

Building a culture of collaboration in the OR requires more than initial efforts—it demands ongoing reinforcement through training, recognition, and leadership. Below are actionable strategies to ensure teamwork remains a priority.

Continuous Training

Collaboration skills, like surgical techniques, need regular refinement.

- Simulation Workshops: Conduct mock surgeries that simulate real-world scenarios, helping teams practice communication and coordination under pressure.
- Teamwork Training: To enhance team dynamics, focus on soft skills such as active listening, conflict resolution, and adaptability.
- Example: A hospital that introduced quarterly simulation workshops saw a 20% improvement in team response times during emergencies.

Recognition Programs

Acknowledging and rewarding collaboration fosters a positive cycle of teamwork and motivation.

Celebrating Success: Highlight teams that consistently achieve collaborative milestones during staff meetings or newsletters.

Incentive Programs: Offer small rewards, such as gift cards or certificates, to recognize outstanding team efforts.

Example: A surgical department celebrated the "Team of the Month" based on turnover efficiency and feedback, boosting morale and friendly competition.

Leadership Support

Leadership sets the tone for collaboration, and OR leaders play a pivotal role in sustaining these efforts.

- **Modeling Behavior:** Leaders should exemplify the collaborative practices they wish to see, such as valuing input from all team members and addressing conflicts promptly.
- **Proactive Problem-Solving:** Regularly review team dynamics and workflows to identify and address potential barriers to collaboration.
- **Example:** OR managers who conducted monthly team check-ins reported higher levels of staff engagement and fewer communication breakdowns.

The Ripple Effect of Collaboration

When hospitals invest in measuring and sustaining collaboration, the results extend beyond the OR. Enhanced teamwork leads to better patient outcomes, greater staff retention, and improved operational efficiency. By embedding collaboration into the DNA of the surgical team, hospitals create a resilient, adaptive environment that thrives under pressure and delivers exceptional care. As healthcare continues to evolve, the ability to work seamlessly as a team will remain a defining factor of success in the OR.

Conclusion

Collaboration is a cornerstone of OR efficiency, impacting patient outcomes, operational performance, and staff satisfaction. Hospitals can create OR environments where collaboration thrives by addressing barriers, leveraging technology, and fostering a culture of teamwork. As the next chapter explores, leadership plays a pivotal role in sustaining these improvements and driving long-term success.

CHAPTER 7

LEADERSHIP'S ROLE IN DRIVING OR EFFICIENCY
Guiding Efficiency, Culture, Innovation, Accountability, & Transformation

---

Introduction

Operating rooms (ORs) are often considered the hospital's lifeline, where clinical precision intersects with operational complexity. However, even with cutting-edge technologies and highly skilled teams, maintaining sustained OR efficiency is nearly impossible without strong, visionary leadership. In this high-stakes environment, leaders are not just administrators but catalysts for change, architects of culture, and champions of continuous improvement. Their ability to unite teams, streamline workflows, and align efforts toward a common goal can mean the difference between success and stagnation.

Leadership in the OR transcends managing schedules and resources—it is about fostering a culture of trust, collaboration, and accountability. Effective leaders inspire their teams to embrace innovation, tackle challenges head-on, and prioritize patient care above all else. They navigate the complexities of surgical operations with strategic foresight, empowering their teams while staying grounded in data-driven decision-making. This chapter explores the profound impact of leadership on OR efficiency, shedding light on the essential qualities, strategies, and tools leaders must employ to drive sustainable improvements.

Through real-world examples, case studies, and actionable insights, this chapter underscores how leadership is not just about directing but enabling. Whether addressing turnover times, implementing new technologies, or fostering collaboration, effective leadership turns operational challenges into opportunities for growth. By setting a clear vision and cultivating an adaptable and resilient team, leaders can transform the OR into a high-performing environment that delivers exceptional outcomes for patients, staff, and the organization.

As we delve deeper into the intricacies of OR leadership, it becomes evident that this role is both an art and a science, requiring a delicate balance of empathy, strategy, and innovation. Through this exploration, we aim to equip current and aspiring leaders with the tools and perspectives needed to excel in one of healthcare's most dynamic arenas.

The Importance of Leadership in OR Efficiency

In the intricate and high-stakes environment of the operating room (OR), leadership is not merely a function—it is the driving force behind operational success. The OR is a space where time is critical, teamwork is non-negotiable, and precision can mean the difference between life and death. In such an environment, effective leadership is the glue that holds processes, people, and technology together, ensuring seamless operations and exceptional patient outcomes.

Leadership in the OR extends beyond managing schedules or ensuring staff punctuality; it requires a strategic vision that aligns every team member and process toward shared goals. Consider a leader who introduces a "Zero Delays" initiative—this is not just about cutting turnover times. It is about fostering a culture where everyone understands their role in eliminating preventable delays, from the cleaning crew preparing the room to the anesthesiologist coordinating with the surgeon. When leadership sets such a clear vision, it creates a unifying purpose that resonates across the team.

Trust and morale are also pivotal in an OR setting. A leader who builds trust among staff fosters an environment where team members feel empowered to voice concerns, share ideas, and collaborate without hesitation. For instance, when a nurse feels comfortable bringing up a potential equipment issue before surgery, it can prevent delays and safeguard patient safety. Open communication, reassuring staff that their contributions are valued, and addressing their concerns are characteristics of strong leadership.

Accountability is another cornerstone of effective OR leadership. In a fast-paced environment, it is easy for tasks to slip through the cracks or for inefficiencies to go unnoticed. Leaders who set clear expectations and regularly review performance ensure that every team member takes ownership of their responsibilities. Imagine an OR where staff receive regular feedback not as a punitive measure but as a tool for improvement. This accountability system drives adherence to protocols, reduces errors, and creates a shared commitment to excellence.

The complexity of OR operations also calls for leaders who can balance immediate operational needs with long-term strategic goals. While addressing daily challenges such as equipment availability or staff shortages, effective leaders invest in initiatives like cross-training programs or advanced technologies that promise sustainable improvements. This dual focus ensures that the OR does not just function efficiently today but is well-positioned to meet the demands of tomorrow.

Ultimately, leadership in the OR is about creating an ecosystem where everyone—from the surgeon to the scrub tech—works cohesively toward a common goal. It is about setting a vision, fostering trust, ensuring accountability, and constantly looking ahead. When leadership excels, the OR transforms from a high-pressure environment into a finely tuned system where efficiency and excellence are the norm, benefiting patients, staff, and the organization.

Essential Leadership Qualities

Leadership in the operating room (OR) requires a unique blend of skills beyond conventional management. The OR's high-stakes, fast-paced nature demands that leaders possess qualities that drive efficiency and foster a supportive and resilient team environment. These essential qualities define leaders who can inspire change, manage complexity, and uphold the highest standards of care.

Strategic Thinking

Every decision in the OR has a ripple effect. Leaders must be able to analyze data, anticipate challenges, and develop forward-thinking plans that align with organizational goals. For example, a leader using predictive analytics to forecast peak surgery times can allocate resources more effectively, ensuring optimal patient care and operational proficiency. Strategic thinkers are proactive, using insights to avoid potential bottlenecks and deficiencies.

Adaptability

The OR is an unpredictable environment where unforeseen issues—equipment malfunctions, last-minute case cancellations, or staff shortages—can arise anytime. Leaders with flexibility can respond to these challenges with composure and creativity. Adaptable leaders do not just react to problems; they prepare for them by having contingency plans and empowering their teams to make informed, real-time decisions. This ability to pivot under pressure ensures continuity and minimizes disruptions.

Empathy and Emotional Intelligence

Understanding OR teams' emotional and physical demands is crucial for effective leadership. Empathy allows leaders to connect with their staff, recognize challenges, and provide meaningful support. A leader who notices signs of burnout and takes proactive steps—such as adjusting schedules or implementing wellness programs—creates a healthier, more engaged workforce. Emotional intelligence helps leaders navigate conflicts, build stronger relationships, and maintain a positive team dynamic under stress.

Communication Skills

Clear, concise, and consistent communication is the backbone of OR operations. Leaders must communicate critical information clearly, leaving no room for misinterpretation. Structured communication tools like Situation, Background, Assessment, Recommendation (SBAR) can standardize the flow of information, reducing errors and enhancing team coordination. A leader who excels in communication builds trust, clears up confusion, and aligns everyone toward shared goals.

Visionary Leadership

Great OR leaders inspire their teams by articulating a compelling vision for the future. Whether adopting cutting-edge technologies, achieving industry-leading efficiency metrics, or creating a culture of excellence, visionary leaders motivate their teams to strive for continuous improvement. Setting ambitious yet attainable goals fosters a sense of purpose and pride that drives the team forward.

Decisiveness

In the OR, hesitation can lead to delays or compromised patient care. Decisive leaders evaluate situations quickly, weigh options effectively, and act with confidence. This quality is essential in emergencies, where timely decisions can save lives and prevent further complications. A decisive leader clarifies uncertain moments, ensuring the team remains focused and cohesive.

Integrity

Trust is paramount in the OR, and leaders who consistently

demonstrate integrity earn the respect and loyalty of their teams. By being honest, transparent, and fair, leaders create an environment where staff feel secure and valued. Integrity ensures that leaders hold themselves and their teams accountable, fostering a culture of mutual respect and reliability.

Resilience

The pressures of managing an OR can be immense, and leaders must exhibit resilience to navigate the highs and lows of their role. Resilient leaders model composure, optimism, and determination, serving as a stabilizing force for their teams during challenging times. Their ability to persevere in adversity inspires confidence and maintains team morale.

By embodying these essential qualities, OR leaders ensure operational success and create a workplace where excellence thrives. These attributes enable leaders to address challenges clearly, inspire their teams to perform at their best, and deliver outstanding patient care.

Leadership Strategies for OR Efficiency

Driving efficiency in the OR requires more than just setting goals; it demands intentional, well-crafted strategies that address the complexities of perioperative care. Effective leaders combine vision, data-driven decision-making, and team empowerment to create an environment where operational excellence thrives. Below are strategies that have proven instrumental in optimizing OR efficiency.

Data-Driven Decision-Making

OR leaders must base their strategies on actionable insights derived from robust data. Metrics such as block utilization rates, turnover times, and surgical site infection rates clearly show where improvements are needed. For example, a hospital leader who used real-time dashboards to monitor OR performance identified bottlenecks in equipment readiness, leading to targeted interventions that reduced delays by 20%.

By prioritizing data, leaders can move beyond anecdotal evidence to implement measurable and impactful changes. This data-driven approach allocates resources effectively, addresses inefficiencies promptly, and drives continuous improvement in outcomes.

Empowering Teams

Empowerment is at the heart of any high-performing OR team. Leaders who delegate responsibilities and foster an environment of trust enable staff to take ownership of their roles. For instance, allowing surgical techs and nurses to identify and address instrument preparation inefficiencies improves workflows and boosts team morale. Empowered teams are more likely to identify potential challenges and propose innovative solutions, fostering a culture of continuous improvement. Leaders can amplify this effect by recognizing and rewarding team-driven initiatives that enhance efficiency and patient care.

Continuous Improvement Initiatives

Adopting methodologies like Lean and Six Sigma allows leaders to tackle inefficiencies systematically. These frameworks focus on reducing waste, standardizing processes, and minimizing workflow variability. A hospital that conducted a Lean process analysis discovered unnecessary steps in its turnover protocol, leading to a 15% reduction in average turnover times. The key to success lies in engaging the entire team during these initiatives. When staff are involved in identifying problems and brainstorming solutions, they are more likely to embrace changes and sustain improvements over time.

Regular Feedback Loops

Leaders who prioritize ongoing feedback create a culture of accountability and adaptability. Post-case debriefings allow teams to reflect on what went well and where improvements are needed.

Similarly, quarterly reviews enable leaders to assess broader trends and implement necessary course corrections. For example, a hospital that implemented structured debriefings after each surgical case saw a 30% decrease in preventable errors within six months. These feedback sessions enhance team performance and demonstrate a leader's commitment to transparency and continuous learning.

Fostering a Collaborative Culture

Collaboration among surgeons, anesthesiologists, nurses, and technicians is essential for OR efficiency. Leaders can foster collaboration by facilitating preoperative briefings and aligning all team members on the surgical plan and potential challenges. A well-communicated plan reduces missteps and enhances the team's ability to respond to unexpected situations.

Through fostering mutual respect and open communication, leaders can dismantle silos and cultivate a unified team that places patient care at the forefront.

Leveraging Technology

Technology is a powerful tool in the leader's arsenal for driving OR efficiency. From real-time dashboards that track turnover times to predictive analytics platforms that optimize scheduling, modern tools enable leaders to make informed decisions quickly. For example, a hospital that integrated AI-driven scheduling software reduced underutilized OR time by 25%, maximizing its surgical capacity. However, successful technology adoption requires careful planning. Leaders must ensure that staff are trained and comfortable with new tools and that the technology integrates seamlessly into existing workflows.

Establishing Clear Goals and Accountability

Leadership in the OR is most effective when driven by a clear vision. Establishing SMART goals (Specific, Measurable, Achievable, Relevant, and Time-bound) for key metrics such as turnover times and case start punctuality provides a roadmap for success. Regularly reviewing progress toward these goals keeps teams focused and motivated.

Accountability is equally important. Leaders must set expectations for team performance and hold individuals responsible for meeting them. At the same time, they should provide the resources and support needed to ensure success.

Prioritizing Staff Well-Being

The high-pressure nature of the OR can lead to burnout and dissatisfaction among staff, which directly impacts efficiency. Leaders who prioritize staff well-being—through initiatives such as wellness programs, flexible scheduling, and professional development opportunities—can mitigate these effects. For instance, a hospital leader who implemented a "Resiliency Program" for perioperative staff saw a marked improvement in team morale, translating to better collaboration and reduced turnover times.

With the application of these leadership strategies, OR leaders can transform their departments into paragons of efficiency and excellence. These methods not only enhance operational performance but also foster a work environment where staff feel valued and motivated, ultimately improving patient care quality. With a clear vision, a focus on collaboration, and an unwavering commitment to continuous improvement, leaders drive the changes necessary to make OR efficiency both achievable and sustainable.

Overcoming Leadership Challenges in the OR

Impactful operating room (OR) leadership is pivotal for achieving efficiency and ensuring optimal patient outcomes. However, even the most experienced leaders face significant challenges in navigating the complexities of the perioperative environment. From resistance to change to resource constraints, these obstacles require proactive strategies and a balanced approach to achieve lasting success.

Below are some of the most pressing leadership challenges and practical solutions.

Resistance to Change

One of the most common challenges in the OR is resistance to change, especially when introducing new workflows, technologies, or efficiency protocols. Change can be perceived as a threat to established routines, creating pushback from staff at all levels.

Challenge: Long-standing habits, fear of the unknown, and skepticism about new systems often lead to hesitation or outright resistance.

Solution: To address this, leaders must engage staff early in the change process. This process involves clear communication about the change's purpose and benefits and openly addressing concerns. For example, during the implementation of a robotic surgery program, leaders at a regional hospital organized town hall meetings where staff could voice concerns and participate in shaping the rollout strategy. Identifying and empowering "change champions" among the staff can also help build momentum and foster trust.

Practical Tip: Provide comprehensive training and pilot programs to ease the transition. When staff sees tangible improvements during trial phases, their confidence and willingness to adopt changes grow significantly.

Balancing Short-Term and Long-Term Goals

Leaders often juggle immediate operational demands with the need to implement long-term strategies for sustained efficiency. This balancing act can create tension and hinder progress if not managed effectively.

Challenge: Focusing too heavily on short-term outcomes can delay critical investments in infrastructure, training, or innovation, while prioritizing long-term goals without addressing current issues may alienate staff or disrupt workflows.

Approach: Data-driven prioritization is key. Leaders should use metrics to identify "quick wins" that demonstrate immediate value while aligning these efforts with broader strategic objectives. For instance, reducing turnover times by five minutes per case may seem incremental, but in a 10-OR hospital, this can save hundreds of hours annually and free resources for other initiatives.

Practical Tip: Establish a phased approach to long-term projects, where early milestones focus on resolving pressing challenges. This approach allows teams to experience tangible progress while building the foundation for more substantial future improvements.

Resource Constraints

Limited budgets and staffing shortages present ongoing challenges for OR leaders, particularly in hospitals serving underserved communities or facing financial pressures.

Problem: Expanding services or upgrading technology may be financially unfeasible, while staffing gaps can increase workloads and exacerbate burnout.

Strategy: Focus on high-yield, low-cost initiatives to maximize the impact of available resources. Cross-training staff to perform multiple roles can enhance flexibility without requiring additional hires. Leaders should also explore creative funding solutions, such as grants, partnerships with technology vendors, or subscription-based models for robotic systems.

Practical Tip: Streamline existing workflows to reduce inefficiencies before investing in new resources. For instance, a Lean analysis of instrument preparation processes can uncover bottlenecks that cost nothing, but yield substantial time savings.

Maintaining Staff Morale in High-Pressure Environments

The OR's fast-paced, high-stakes nature can lead to stress, burnout, and dissatisfaction among staff, all of which negatively impact team performance and efficiency.

Insight: Overworked and undervalued staff are less likely to collaborate effectively or embrace new initiatives, creating a cycle of inefficiency and disengagement.

Action: Recognize the human element of OR operations by prioritizing staff well-being. This prioritization can include offering flexible scheduling, implementing wellness programs, and fostering a culture of appreciation. For instance, a hospital leader who launched a monthly 'Excellence in Perioperative Care' award observed a significant boost in team morale and collaboration.

Practical Tip: Solicit regular feedback from staff to understand their pain points and address them proactively. Whether it is adjusting shift patterns or providing ergonomic equipment, slight changes can significantly impact satisfaction and retention.

Navigating Interdisciplinary Conflicts

The OR brings together diverse professionals—surgeons, anesthesiologists, nurses, and technicians, each with distinct roles and perspectives. Misaligned goals or miscommunications can lead to conflicts that disrupt workflows.

Challenge: Conflicts often stem from unclear roles, misunderstandings about priorities, or unequal workload distribution.

Approach: Establishing standardized communication protocols, such as preoperative briefings and structured handoffs, can mitigate conflicts by ensuring everyone is on the same page. Leaders should also facilitate team-building activities to strengthen interpersonal relationships and foster mutual respect.

Practical Tip: Leaders must act as mediators when conflicts arise, addressing issues promptly and impartially. Training in conflict resolution techniques can prepare leaders to manage tensions effectively without alienating team members.

Technology Fatigue

While technology is a powerful enabler of OR efficiency, over-reliance on it can lead to "technology fatigue," where staff feel overwhelmed by new tools or overly dependent on automation.

Observation: When systems fail or require updates, staff overly reliant on technology may struggle to adapt, causing delays.

Solution: Leaders should balance technology adoption with hands-on training and manual workflow planning. For example, while implementing an AI-driven scheduling system, a hospital ensured all staff were proficient in manual scheduling as a backup.

Practical Tip: Encourage a culture of continuous learning where staff are comfortable adapting to technological and non-technological solutions.

Anticipating and tackling these leadership challenges allows OR leaders to cultivate a resilient environment where efficiency flourishes. Achieving success demands a strategic vision, empathy, adaptability, and a dedication to supporting the teams that make excellence in the OR a reality.

Case Study: Leadership-Driven Transformation in the OR

Situation: A regional hospital with a 10-OR facility faced high turnover times, frequent delays, and declining staff morale.

Task: Revamp OR operations by implementing leadership-driven efficiency initiatives.

Action:
1. Introduced a data dashboard to track key metrics like turnover times and block utilization.
2. Conducted biweekly staff meetings to gather feedback and provide updates on progress.
3. Launched a recognition program to celebrate team achievements in meeting efficiency targets.

Result:
- Turnover times were reduced by 18% within six months.
- Staff satisfaction scores improved by 35%.
- Increased OR utilization by 12%, generating an additional $2 million in annual revenue.

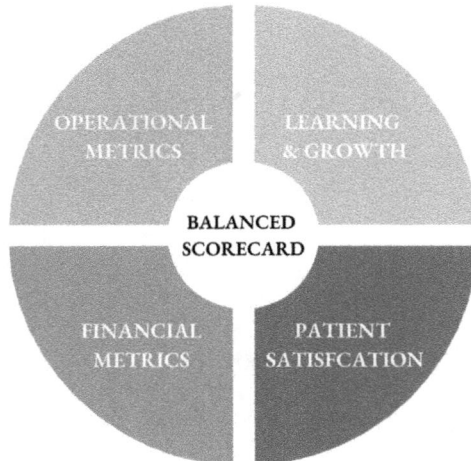

Tools and Frameworks for Leadership

Leaders can leverage various tools and frameworks to enhance OR efficiency:

Balanced Scorecard

The Balanced Scorecard is a strategic management tool that tracks performance across four critical dimensions: financial outcomes, operational processes, learning and growth, and customer (patient) satisfaction. It provides a comprehensive view of an organization's performance, ensuring alignment between OR-specific objectives and broader organizational goals.

Key Elements:

- Financial Metrics: Measures cost per case, resource utilization, and revenue generated from OR procedures.
- Operational Metrics: Tracks first-case on-time starts, turnover times, and cancellations.
- Learning and Growth: Focuses on staff training, skill development, and innovation adoption.
- Patient Satisfaction: Assesses the outcomes, safety metrics, and patient feedback on the surgical experience.

Example: A large healthcare system implemented a Balanced Scorecard to monitor OR efficiency across multiple facilities. By tracking the turnover time reduction initiative, they identified bottlenecks in equipment availability and streamlined the CSPD (Central Sterile Processing Department) workflows. Over six months, the organization saw a 15% reduction in turnover times and significant improvements in staff satisfaction.

Leadership Rounds

Leadership rounds involve regular visits by leaders (such as perioperative directors, nurse managers, and medical executives) to the OR to observe workflows, engage with staff, and identify opportunities for improvement.

Purpose:

- Build trust and foster collaboration between leadership and frontline staff.
- Gain firsthand insights into challenges, inefficiencies, and morale issues.
- Demonstrate commitment to resolving issues and improving the working environment.

Benefits:

- It enhances communication and creates a culture of openness.
- Promotes early identification of operational challenges, such as equipment delays or staffing gaps.
- Encourages staff ownership of OR efficiency initiatives.

Example: At a leading hospital, leadership rounds uncovered a recurring issue with delays caused by incomplete surgical kits. Leaders engaged directly with CSPD staff during rounds and initiated a standardization process for preference cards, reducing errors by 40% within three months.

Change Management Models

Implementing change in the high-pressure operating room (OR) environment requires a structured and thoughtful approach. Change management models offer frameworks that help leaders introduce new processes, technologies, and cultural shifts while minimizing resistance and ensuring long-term success. These models provide a roadmap for navigating the complexities of OR dynamics and fostering collaboration among diverse teams.

The Need for Structured Change

Change in the OR is inevitable, whether driven by technological advancements, evolving patient needs, or efficiency goals. However, even well-intentioned initiatives can face resistance or fail to deliver results without proper planning. Structured change management models address this challenge by providing clear steps to guide leaders and teams through the transition. They help align stakeholders, maintain morale, and ensure that new practices are implemented and sustained over time.

Kotter's 8-Step Model: Building Momentum

One of the most popular frameworks for managing change is Kotter's 8-Step Model, which emphasizes creating urgency and building momentum. In an OR setting, this model identifies inefficiencies—such as high turnover times or frequent delays—and demonstrates the need for immediate action. Leaders can drive the change process collaboratively by forming a coalition of champions from across surgical teams.

CREATE
A SENSE OF URGENCY

INSTITUTE
CHANGE

BUILD
A GUIDING COALITION

SUSTAIN
ACCELERATION

THE BIG opportunity

FORM
A STRATEGIC VISION

GENERATE
SHORT-TERM WINS

ENABLE
ACTION BY REMOVING BARRIERS

ENLIST
A VOLUNTEER ARMY

For instance, when a hospital introduced robotic-assisted surgery, leaders followed Kotter's Model to address initial resistance. They created a sense of urgency by highlighting patient outcomes and competitive advantages, then empowered change champions to advocate for the technology. Regular wins, such as successful pilot cases, helped sustain momentum.

ADKAR Model: Focusing on Individuals

The ADKAR Model is particularly effective in the OR, emphasizing individual change. This framework breaks the process into five key elements: Awareness, Desire, Knowledge, Ability, and Reinforcement. By addressing the unique concerns of each team member, this Model ensures that no one feels left behind.

A
Awareness
Of the need for change

D
Desire
To participate and support the change

K
Knowledge
On how to change

A
Ability
To implement required skills & behaviors

R
Reinforcement
To sustain the change

For example, during the transition to AI-based scheduling tools, a hospital used the ADKAR model to tailor training sessions for nurses, surgeons, and anesthesiologists. Awareness sessions outlined the benefits, while hands-on training addressed gaps in knowledge and ability. Regular feedback loops reinforced the new workflows, ensuring long-term adoption.

Lewin's Change Management Model: A Simplified Approach
For leaders seeking a straightforward framework, Lewin's Change Management Model offers a three-stage process: Unfreeze, Change, and Refreeze. In the OR, this might involve unfreezing old habits by identifying bottlenecks in current workflows, introducing new practices such as staggered scheduling, and reinforcing these changes through ongoing audits and rewards.

Solidify the change as the new norm by reinforcing and embedding it into the organizational culture to prevent regression.

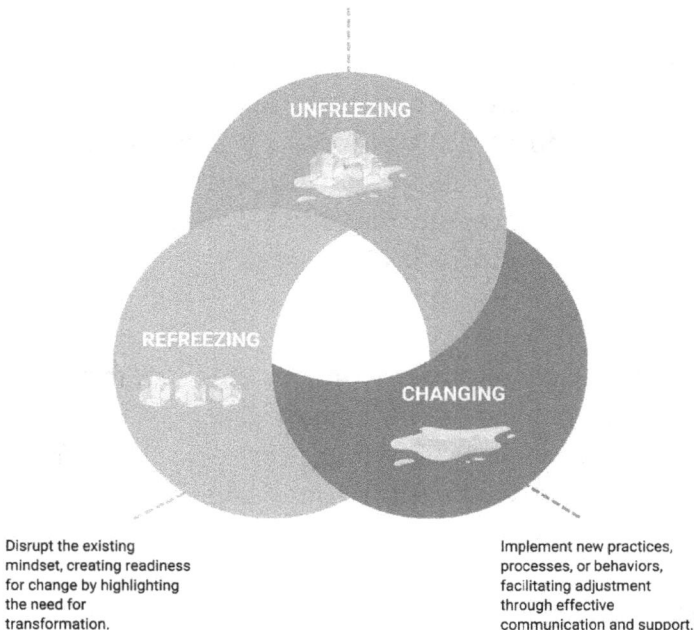

UNFREEZING

REFREEZING

CHANGING

Disrupt the existing mindset, creating readiness for change by highlighting the need for transformation.

Implement new practices, processes, or behaviors, facilitating adjustment through effective communication and support.

This model proved effective for hospitals in addressing delays in surgical kit preparation. By unfreezing existing processes through a Lean analysis, introducing standardized preference cards, and refreezing the new system with clear accountability measures, the hospital reduced preparation delays by 40%.

Engaging Stakeholders for Success

Regardless of the Model used, engaging stakeholders is critical. Change in the OR affects multiple disciplines, and success hinges on aligning their goals. Leaders must communicate the "why" behind each initiative and involve team members in shaping the solution. Open forums, one-on-one meetings, and pilot programs can build trust and buy-in. For instance, when introducing preoperative briefings, a hospital held focus groups to gather input from surgeons, nurses, and technicians. By incorporating their feedback, the leadership team ensured the change met everyone's needs, leading to enthusiastic adoption.

Sustaining Change Through Leadership

Sustaining change requires ongoing leadership support. Leaders must model the desired behaviors, celebrate milestones, and address challenges promptly. Reinforcement is vital in the OR, where high-pressure situations tempt staff to revert to old habits. Leaders can embed new practices into the culture by consistently emphasizing the benefits and addressing concerns.

Through strategic use of change management models, OR leaders can navigate the complexities of implementation, foster team collaboration, and achieve lasting improvements. Whether adopting cutting-edge technologies or refining workflows, these frameworks provide the tools needed to transform challenges into opportunities for growth.

Lean and Six Sigma Tools: Streamlining OR Efficiency

Lean and Six Sigma methodologies have become indispensable in modern healthcare, offering a systematic approach to reducing waste, minimizing variability, and enhancing workflow efficiency. In the operating room (OR), where time and precision are critical, these tools empower leaders and teams to identify bottlenecks, eliminate redundancies, and create a seamless environment for surgical care. Their application is not merely about efficiency—it is about fostering a culture of continuous improvement that aligns with the overarching goals of patient safety, staff satisfaction, and financial sustainability.

What Are Lean and Six Sigma?
Lean methodology reduces process waste, ensuring every step adds value. Six Sigma emphasizes reducing defects and variability through data-driven analysis. Together, these approaches create a robust framework for optimizing OR workflows.

For example, a hospital struggling with frequent turnover delays applied Lean principles to streamline equipment preparation and used Six Sigma tools to analyze and resolve root causes. This dual approach reduced delays by 25%, significantly increasing OR utilization.

Process Mapping: Visualizing Efficiency
One of the foundational tools in Lean methodology is process mapping, a visual representation of workflows that helps teams identify inefficiencies. In the OR, process mapping can uncover redundancies in equipment setup, cleaning protocols, or communication handoffs.

Consider a perioperative team mapping out the journey of surgical instruments from the Central Sterile Processing Department (CSPD) to the OR. By identifying unnecessary steps and streamlining the handoff process, the team reduced instrument preparation delays by 15%, ensuring surgeries started on time.

LEAN APPROACH

Pull
Velocity
One Piece Flow
Value Stream Mapping

COMMON OBJECTIVE

Variability Reduction
Cycle Time Reduction
Customer Satisfaction

SIX SIGMA APPROACH

Statistical Methods
Design of Experiments
Statistical Process Control
Defects Per Million Opportunities

DMAIC: A Roadmap for Improvement

Six Sigma's DMAIC framework—Define, Measure, Analyze, Improve, Control—is particularly effective for tackling complex OR challenges. This structured methodology ensures that every change is backed by data and aligned with organizational goals.

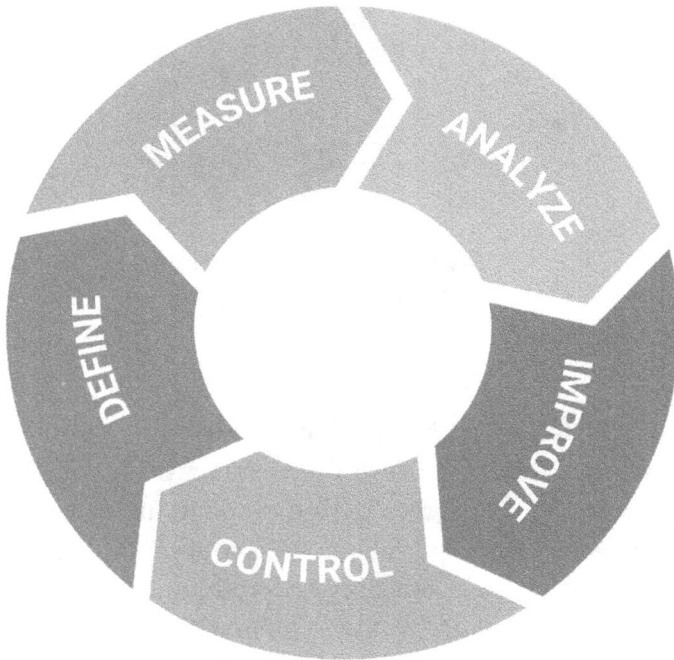

For instance, a hospital experiencing high rates of case cancellations used DMAIC to address the issue. During the "Define" phase, they identified cancellations due to incomplete preoperative documentation. In the "Measure" and "Analyze" phases, they tracked error rates and pinpointed gaps in communication between surgeons and administrative staff. By implementing electronic reminders during the "Improve" phase and monitoring adherence during the "Control" phase, the hospital reduced cancellations by 30%.

5S Methodology: Organizing the OR

The 5S methodology—Sort, Set in Order, Shine, Standardize, Sustain—is another Lean tool that directly impacts OR efficiency. By organizing the surgical environment, 5S minimizes time spent searching for instruments, reduces errors, and creates a safer workspace.

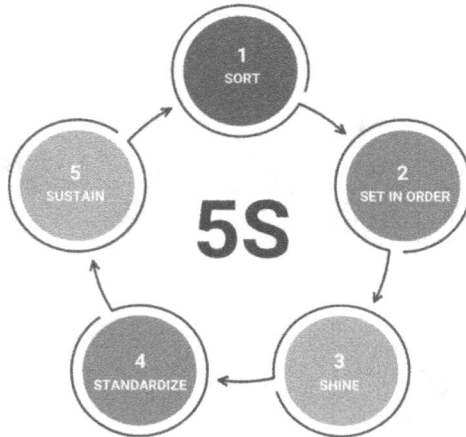

Reducing Variability with Standard Work

Standard work, a Lean tool, creates consistency in task performance, reducing variability and errors. This tool might include standardizing cleaning protocols, equipment setup procedures, or preoperative briefings in the OR. A teaching hospital implemented standard work for preoperative nursing assessments, ensuring every patient received the same level of care. This not only improved patient outcomes but also reduced variability in preparation times, enhancing overall efficiency.

Creating a Culture of Continuous Improvement

The true power of Lean and Six Sigma lies in their ability to foster a mindset of continuous improvement. OR teams trained in these methodologies are better equipped to identify inefficiencies and propose solutions proactively. Hospitals can ensure that efficiency gains are sustained over time by encouraging staff to take ownership of process improvement.

Leadership plays a critical role in this transformation. Regular Kaizen events—dedicated sessions for process improvement—engage multidisciplinary teams in brainstorming and testing new ideas. For example, one hospital used a Kaizen event to address recurring delays in transferring post-anesthesia care unit (PACU) patients. The team's solutions reduced transfer delays by 20%, freeing up ORs for incoming cases.

Impact Beyond the OR

Lean and Six Sigma principles extend beyond the OR, creating ripple effects across the healthcare system. Improved efficiency in the OR translates to better patient flow, reduced wait times, and enhanced financial performance. Hospitals that adopt these tools achieve immediate gains and position themselves for long-term success in an increasingly competitive healthcare landscape.

By integrating Lean and Six Sigma tools into their operations, OR leaders can transform inefficiencies into opportunities, ensuring that every process is as streamlined and effective as possible. The result is an environment where patient care thrives, staff are empowered, and resources are optimized—a true win for everyone involved.

The Long-Term Impact of Leadership

Effective leadership in the operating room (OR) does more than deliver short-term operational gains; it creates a ripple effect that drives sustained organizational success. When leaders embrace efficiency and foster a culture of collaboration and accountability, the long-term benefits extend far beyond the OR walls.

Below are the key long-term impacts of effective leadership:

Cultural Shift

Leadership is critical in fostering a cultural shift that embeds efficiency and excellence into an organization's fabric. In the high-pressure operating room (OR) environment, where even minor inefficiencies can cascade into significant issues, a culture centered on continuous improvement transforms workflows and team dynamics. When leaders champion values like accountability, ownership, and collaboration, they create an ecosystem where everyone feels responsible for achieving operational excellence. This shift is about implementing policies and inspiring individuals to embrace efficiency as a shared goal.

Empowering team members to take ownership of OR efficiency is a cornerstone of cultural transformation. When staff feel their contributions are recognized and valued, they are more likely to actively engage in problem-solving and process optimization. For instance, a nurse who notices recurring delays in equipment preparation is more likely to propose actionable solutions in a culture that values their input. This sense of ownership creates a ripple effect, where individuals at all levels proactively seek ways to improve, leading to a more efficient and harmonious environment.

Transparency is another critical element of cultural change. Open communication channels foster trust, making it easier for staff to report inefficiencies or suggest improvements without fear of blame. Leaders prioritizing transparency encourage a collaborative approach to addressing challenges, ensuring that teams work together to find practical solutions. This environment of mutual respect improves morale and helps identify systemic issues that may otherwise go unnoticed.

A strong leadership presence also ensures accountability becomes a core value within the OR. Clear expectations, regular feedback, and recognition motivate staff to uphold high-performance standards. Consider the example of a large academic hospital implementing a recognition program to celebrate staff contributions to OR efficiency. The hospital reduced equipment-related delays by 25% over two years by shifting the focus from reactive problem-solving to proactive ownership. This example underscores how a leadership-driven cultural shift can result in sustained improvements, benefiting staff and patients.

Enhanced Reputation

A high-performing operating room (OR) is more than a cornerstone of surgical excellence—a defining feature of a hospital's reputation. Efficiency, innovation, and patient-centered care send a strong message about the institution's commitment to excellence. Leadership is pivotal in building this reputation by fostering an environment prioritizing quality outcomes, operational efficiency, and staff well-being. A well-regarded OR becomes a competitive advantage, attracting top-tier professionals and earning the trust of patients and their families.

Hospitals with well-managed ORs are magnets for skilled professionals. Institutions prioritizing efficiency attract surgeons, anesthesiologists, and nurses, allowing them to focus on delivering exceptional care instead of navigating avoidable delays. Moreover, OR staff satisfaction tends to increase when leadership invests in resources such as cutting-edge technology, robust training programs, and opportunities for professional development. These investments create a cycle of excellence, as a satisfied team performs better, further enhancing the hospital's reputation and reducing costly turnover rates.

From the patient's perspective, an efficient OR translates into shorter wait times, timely surgeries, and improved outcomes—all factors that inspire trust and confidence. Patients are increasingly savvy about their healthcare choices, often relying on online reviews, word-of-mouth, and publicized hospital metrics. A strong OR reputation can differentiate a hospital in a crowded market, making it a preferred choice for elective surgeries or complex procedures. Efficiency in the OR becomes a tangible representation of the hospital's broader commitment to quality care.

Consider the case of a regional medical center that transformed its OR operations by adopting robotic-assisted surgery and streamlining turnover times. These innovations, driven by a forward-thinking leadership team, significantly reduced delays and improved surgical outcomes. Over five years, the hospital saw a 30% increase in patient referrals, as its reputation as a leading surgical center attracted not only patients but also high-acuity cases that brought financial and clinical prestige.

Ultimately, an enhanced OR reputation is not just about external perception—it reflects internal excellence. When leadership prioritizes efficiency and collaboration, it creates a culture that thrives on delivering value at every level. This culture of continuous improvement ensures that patients receive high-quality care while the hospital strengthens its position in the competitive healthcare market. The ripple effects of a strong OR reputation extend far beyond the surgical suite, impacting everything from patient satisfaction scores to long-term financial sustainability.

Financial Resilience
ORs are typically one of the most significant revenue-generating departments in any hospital. Effective leadership ensures operational efficiencies translate into financial sustainability, enabling the organization to reinvest in people, technology, and infrastructure.

Cost Savings:
- Reducing turnover times, optimizing staffing, and preventing case cancellations directly lower operational costs.
- For example, decreasing turnover time by just five minutes per case in a hospital with ten ORs performing ten surgeries daily can save hundreds of thousands of dollars annually.

Revenue Growth:
- Increased efficiency allows more surgeries within the same time frame, boosting procedural volume and associated revenue.
- Hospitals with efficient ORs can take on higher acuity, higher-reimbursement cases.

Investment in Sustainability:
- Financial resilience enables reinvestment in critical areas, such as staff training, cutting-edge technology, and facility upgrades.

Example: Under new leadership, a hospital experiencing high cancellation rates revamped its scheduling process and invested in predictive analytics tools. The resulting 20% increase in case volume added millions of dollars in annual revenue, providing the resources for continued innovation.

Building an Adaptive Organization
Adaptability is the hallmark of a successful operating room (OR) in the ever-evolving healthcare landscape. Effective leaders foster flexibility and resilience, ensuring their teams can navigate challenges and seize growth opportunities. The ability to respond swiftly to unforeseen circumstances or industry shifts is not just advantageous—it is essential for long-term sustainability.

Scalable Processes are an essential element of adaptability. By standardizing workflows and documentation across multiple ORs, hospitals can streamline operations during periods of growth or reorganization. Scalable systems ensure that efficiency and quality are maintained even as demand fluctuates, providing a consistent standard of care.

Data-driven decision-making empowers leaders to anticipate challenges and adjust strategies accordingly. Monitoring key performance metrics allows organizations to identify emerging trends and proactively address inefficiencies. For example, hospitals that leverage predictive analytics can better allocate resources during peak surgical periods, avoiding bottlenecks and delays.

Cross-training staff is a vital strategy for fostering flexibility. OR teams trained in multiple roles are better equipped to handle unexpected shortages or surges in demand. This approach ensures operational continuity and enhances team cohesion and morale, as staff members feel empowered to contribute to various capacities.

An example of adaptability in action occurred during the COVID-19 pandemic when hospitals with efficient and flexible OR systems successfully repurposed staff and resources to support critical care needs. Leadership invested in resilience before the crisis minimized disruptions, highlighting the importance of preparedness in an unpredictable environment. This adaptability is a testament to the value of forward-thinking leadership in building sustainable and agile healthcare systems.

Fostering Innovation

Innovation is the driving force behind advancements in operating room (OR) efficiency, and strong leadership is essential to nurturing a culture that embraces change. Leaders who foster creativity and openness to innovative ideas position their OR teams to tackle complex challenges with creative solutions.

This commitment to innovation improves patient care and ensures that the OR remains a hub of progress in the healthcare system.

One key area of innovation is the adoption of robotic surgery platforms. These systems enhance surgical precision, reduce recovery times, and expand the possibilities for minimally invasive procedures. By introducing robotic technology, leaders can transform their OR capabilities, offering patients safer and more efficient surgical options while improving outcomes across various specialties.

Another transformative innovation is the use of AI and predictive analytics. These tools enable ORs to optimize scheduling, forecast demand, and accurately predict patient outcomes. By leveraging real-time data, leaders can reduce delays, improve resource allocation, and ensure smooth workflows, making every surgical day more predictable and efficient.

Telemedicine and virtual support represent another groundbreaking advancement. By integrating remote consultations into preoperative and post-operative care, hospitals can improve patient flow and reduce the burden on physical facilities. Telemedicine also ensures continuity of care for patients in rural or underserved areas, broadening access to specialized surgical expertise.

For example, a hospital implementing a real-time dashboard monitoring system achieved remarkable results. The dashboard identified inefficiencies in equipment turnover and enabled immediate corrective actions, increasing daily OR throughput by 15%. This innovation streamlined operations and reinforced the importance of adopting data-driven solutions to address real-time challenges.

Through bold leadership and a commitment to progress, fostering innovation ensures that OR teams stay ahead of the curve, continuously improving efficiency, patient outcomes, and overall operational excellence.

Conclusion

Leadership is the cornerstone of achieving and sustaining efficiency in the operating room (OR). Leaders can navigate challenges and implement lasting change by setting a clear vision, fostering a culture of continuous improvement, and empowering teams to take ownership. Effective leadership transforms the OR from a high-pressure environment into a cohesive, well-oiled system that delivers exceptional patient care.

A successful leader combines strategic foresight with hands-on engagement, leveraging data-driven strategies to identify bottlenecks, streamline workflows, and measure outcomes. This balance between vision and execution creates an environment where innovation and adaptability thrive, ensuring the OR remains agile despite evolving healthcare demands.

The impact of leadership extends beyond operational gains—it shapes culture, strengthens reputation, and ensures financial resilience. Leaders who remain focused on the patient and the broader organizational mission are instrumental in driving sustainable success.

As the next chapter explores the financial aspects of OR operations, it becomes clear that understanding and optimizing the OR's economic drivers is just as vital for ensuring long-term growth and sustainability.

CHAPTER 8

FINANCIAL IMPLICATIONS OF OR EFFICIENCY
Balancing Costs, Revenue, and Quality

Introduction
The operating room (OR) is more than just a place for surgeries—it is the financial engine of any hospital. Operating rooms commonly account for over 60% of a hospital's revenue, so their efficiency directly impacts the institution's fiscal health. However, this comes with high stakes: inefficiencies in OR management can quickly escalate costs, disrupt operations, and diminish profitability.

OR proficiency is not merely about running on time or minimizing delays, but also understanding the broader financial picture. Every decision, from scheduling and staffing to equipment utilization, carries financial consequences. This chapter provides a detailed roadmap for recognizing and addressing the economic implications of OR efficiency, enabling hospital leaders to drive both clinical excellence and financial sustainability.

The OR's Role in Hospital Finances
Operating rooms are unique in their dual role as revenue generators and cost centers. This duality makes their efficient management critical for maintaining financial balance.

Revenue Generation: ORs are a primary source of income, mainly through high-margin elective procedures and complex cases. Elective surgeries, such as joint replacements or bariatric procedures, often attract commercially insured patients, boosting revenue. Complex cases, like cardiac or neurosurgical procedures, bring in substantial reimbursements due to their specialized nature and high resource demand.

Cost Centers: Despite being revenue drivers, ORs are among the most expensive hospital units. Labor costs form the most significant expense, encompassing salaries for surgeons, anesthesiologists, nurses, and support staff. Supply costs, including surgical instruments and implants, represent another significant financial burden, often requiring precise forecasting and management to avoid waste. Capital investments, such as purchasing robotic systems or advanced imaging tools, also demand high initial funding and consistent utilization to ensure a return on investment.

Key Insight: While ORs offer immense earning potential, inefficiencies such as idle time, underutilized blocks, or unplanned cancellations can quickly erode margins, highlighting the need to streamline operations.

The Cost of Inefficiencies

Inefficiencies in OR operations have far-reaching consequences, impacting direct costs and lost revenue opportunities. Here's how specific inefficiencies manifest and what they cost hospitals:

Idle Time: Underused OR time is one of the most significant drains on resources. For example, a hospital that averages 20 minutes of idle time per surgery risks losing hundreds of thousands in potential annual revenue—the costs compound when idle ORs waste staffing resources, energy, and equipment readiness.

Delays and Cancellations: Last-minute cancellations are not just an inconvenience—they are a financial setback. Canceled cases waste staff wages, equipment preparation costs, and other operational expenses. Moreover, rescheduling these cases adds further strain to OR schedules. Implementing robust preoperative assessment protocols can significantly reduce these instances.

Extended Turnover Times: Turnover inefficiencies prevent the OR from maximizing its surgical throughput. For example, a hospital that reduces turnover by 10 minutes per case could perform an additional 200 procedures annually. If each case generates $10,000 in revenue, that is $2 million in incremental income.

Supply Waste: Excess or expired inventory leads to unnecessary costs. Surgical items that are opened but unused during procedures often must be discarded. A well-managed inventory system with regular audits and just-in-time supply chains can mitigate this waste.

Illustrative Example: A tertiary hospital faced losses of $1.2 million annually due to equipment turnover and scheduling inefficiencies. Addressing these issues reduced waste and significantly improved their bottom line.

Strategies for Cost Optimization
To address financial inefficiencies, hospitals can implement targeted strategies that optimize spending without compromising care quality.

Streamlining Supply Chains: Centralized procurement allows hospitals to negotiate better vendor contracts, secure bulk discounts, and reduce per-unit costs. Additionally, leveraging data analytics to predict supply needs ensures that materials are neither over-ordered nor understocked. This approach reduces both waste and delays caused by missing items.

Reducing Overtime Costs: Over-reliance on overtime stems from mismatched staffing schedules and unexpected case volumes. Hospitals can alleviate this issue by creating flexible staffing models, cross-training staff to handle multiple roles, and aligning schedules with forecasted surgical demand.

Improving Equipment Utilization: Strategic scheduling of high-value assets like robotic systems maximizes usage during peak hours. Staggering robotic case schedules ensures consistent utilization, reduces downtime, and boosts the financial return on these investments.

Enhancing Turnover Efficiency: Every minute saved in turnover can lead to additional revenue opportunities. Hospitals can streamline this process by training staff in synchronized cleaning protocols, introducing automated cleaning tools, and enforcing standardized turnover checklists.

Revenue Growth Opportunities

Beyond controlling costs, efficient ORs can unlock significant revenue potential by capitalizing on existing resources.

Maximizing Block Utilization: Underutilized blocks represent missed opportunities. AI-powered scheduling platforms optimize OR time allocation, matching demand with capacity and minimizing schedule gaps.

Expanding High-Demand Services: Hospitals can enhance profitability by offering specialized procedures, such as minimally invasive surgeries, which attract high reimbursements. Expanding service lines to include emerging areas like robotic surgery or bariatric care can also capture new patient demographics.

Reducing Patient Leakage: Patient leakage represents a significant financial loss when referred patients seek care outside the hospital system. Patient navigation programs and improved care coordination can help retain these patients, ensuring that referrals translate into completed cases.

Optimizing Payer Mix: Hospitals can strategically attract commercially insured patients through targeted marketing and partnerships. Developing bundled payment models aligns hospital incentives with payer priorities, creating mutually beneficial outcomes.

Measuring Financial Performance in the OR

To evaluate the success of efficiency initiatives, hospitals must track specific financial and operational KPIs:

- Cost per Case: Helps identify high-cost procedures and areas for expense reduction.
- Block Utilization Rate: Measures the percentage of allocated OR time used, highlighting scheduling efficiency.
- Turnover Time: Tracks the average time between surgeries, offering insights into operational delays.
- Revenue per OR Hour: Indicates the financial productivity of each operating room.

These metrics enable leadership to make data-driven decisions, prioritize improvement efforts, and measure the return on investment for implemented strategies.

Balancing Cost and Quality

While financial efficiency is crucial, it should never come at the expense of patient care.

Hospitals must strike a balance by:

- Investing in Quality: Allocating resources to infection control, staff training, and advanced equipment ensures that patient outcomes remain a top priority.

- Aligning Incentives: Linking staff bonuses to efficiency and quality metrics fosters a culture of accountability without compromising care standards.
- Focusing on Sustainability: Short-term cost-cutting measures often lead to long-term inefficiencies. Strategic investments in technology and training yield better outcomes over time.

Conclusion

The financial implications of operating room (OR) efficiency extend beyond the immediate boundaries of surgical workflows, impacting the hospital's financial health, reputation, and ability to deliver high-quality care. Efficient OR management is not merely an operational goal, but an economic imperative that aligns with the broader mission of patient-centered care. Hospitals can unlock cost savings and generate additional revenue by addressing inefficiencies such as idle time, turnover delays, and supply waste, reinforcing their ability to invest in innovation, technology, and workforce development. The financial gains from improved OR proficiency empower institutions to better navigate the complexities of modern healthcare.

Achieving financial sustainability in the operating room requires more than just operational changes—it involves balancing cost control with maintaining high-quality care. Hospitals that focus on both patient outcomes and strategic resource utilization are better positioned to succeed in competitive healthcare markets. Strong leadership is essential for finding this balance, driving the use of innovative tools, fostering a culture of accountability, and ensuring that financial goals do not undermine clinical excellence. By connecting financial metrics with quality indicators like patient satisfaction and safety, hospitals can create a cohesive approach to OR management that benefits all stakeholders.

The path to financial sustainability in the OR is a journey of continuous improvement. Hospitals must embrace data-driven strategies, adaptive leadership, and team collaboration to maintain efficiency and resilience. As a financial powerhouse, the operating room can lead the way in transforming healthcare delivery, setting the stage for sustainable growth and excellence. The next chapter examines the role of data analytics, revealing how actionable insights can further enhance OR performance and drive long-term success.

CHAPTER 9

LEVERAGING DATA ANALYTICS FOR OR EXCELLENCE
Transforming Decisions Through Surgical Insights

Introduction

In the fast-paced world of healthcare, the operating room (OR) serves as both a critical clinical environment and a substantial revenue generator. Data analytics has emerged as a powerful tool that revolutionizes decision-making and operational efficiency. Whether optimizing scheduling, streamlining turnover times, or managing surgical supply chains, analytics offers actionable insights that allow healthcare teams to anticipate challenges, implement targeted solutions, and deliver exceptional patient care.

This chapter investigates the transformative impact of data analytics in achieving excellence in the operating room. In addition to improving performance, analytics enables hospitals to align with value-based care models, cutting costs while enhancing clinical outcomes. Through the exploration of real-world applications, key performance indicators, and the latest tools, we uncover how hospitals can fully leverage data-driven strategies to foster a more innovative and adaptable OR environment.

The integration of data analytics into surgical workflows is not without challenges. However, with careful implementation, training, and the right technology, hospitals can overcome these barriers and lay the groundwork for sustained improvement. As we progress through this chapter, we examine how data analytics reshapes OR operations and sets a new standard for healthcare innovation.

The Role of Data Analytics in OR Efficiency

Data analytics has transformed how hospitals approach operating room (OR) management by providing actionable insights that drive efficiency, enhance decision-making, and improve patient outcomes. With its ability to uncover hidden inefficiencies, forecast challenges, and optimize workflows, analytics empowers healthcare leaders to make informed decisions that align operational goals with clinical and financial success.

Enhanced Decision-Making

In a high-stakes environment like the OR, split-second decisions can significantly impact patient outcomes and hospital operations. Data analytics equips surgical teams and administrators with real-time dashboards that track critical metrics such as turnover times, case durations, and resource utilization. For example, a large hospital implementing a data-driven monitoring system reduced idle time by 15%, ensuring that ORs were used optimally throughout the day. These real-time insights allow leaders to proactively identify bottlenecks, address delays, and allocate resources more effectively. Whether reassigning staff to high-demand areas or adjusting schedules to account for unexpected emergencies, data-driven decisions reduce downtime and improve overall operational flow.

Predictive Capabilities

Analytics does not just reveal what is happening—it forecasts what is likely to occur. Predictive algorithms analyze historical data to anticipate patient volumes, surgical demand, and resource needs. This foresight allows hospitals to prepare adequately, minimizing the risk of scheduling conflicts or last-minute cancellations. For instance, predictive scheduling tools can identify trends in surgeon availability and patient preferences, ensuring block utilization maximization without overburdening staff. A Midwest hospital implementing such tools saw a 25% reduction in underutilized OR blocks, improving patient access and financial performance.

Performance Monitoring

Maintaining long-term OR performance relies on ongoing evaluation, and data analytics offers a robust framework for monitoring key metrics over time. By tracking performance indicators such as turnover times, block utilization rates, and on-time starts for the first case, hospitals can identify areas for improvement and implement focused interventions. For instance, a perioperative team using analytics to assess adherence to scheduled start times discovered frequent delays in pre-surgical preparations. After addressing the underlying causes, they improved first-case on-time starts by 20%, resulting in better patient satisfaction and more predictable operations.

Broader Impacts on Accountability

Data analytics also fosters accountability by making performance visible at every level of the surgical team. Surgeons, nurses, and support staff can track their impact on OR performance, fostering a culture where everyone is committed to continuous improvement. For hospital administrators, analytics provides evidence-based insights, making it easier to justify resource allocation and strategic decisions. In the OR, where every second counts and inefficiencies can have significant consequences; data analytics is an essential tool for achieving operational excellence. Empowering leaders and teams with timely, accurate information bridges the gap between clinical priorities and operational goals, creating a high-performing surgical environment.

The integration of data analytics into surgical workflows is not without challenges. However, with careful implementation, training, and the right technology, hospitals can overcome these barriers and lay the groundwork for sustained improvement. As we progress through this chapter, we examine how data analytics reshapes OR operations and sets a new standard for healthcare innovation.

The Role of Data Analytics in OR Efficiency

Data analytics has transformed how hospitals approach operating room (OR) management by providing actionable insights that drive efficiency, enhance decision-making, and improve patient outcomes. With its ability to uncover hidden inefficiencies, forecast challenges, and optimize workflows, analytics empowers healthcare leaders to make informed decisions that align operational goals with clinical and financial success.

Enhanced Decision-Making

In a high-stakes environment like the OR, split-second decisions can significantly impact patient outcomes and hospital operations. Data analytics equips surgical teams and administrators with real-time dashboards that track critical metrics such as turnover times, case durations, and resource utilization. For example, a large hospital implementing a data-driven monitoring system reduced idle time by 15%, ensuring that ORs were used optimally throughout the day. These real-time insights allow leaders to proactively identify bottlenecks, address delays, and allocate resources more effectively. Whether reassigning staff to high-demand areas or adjusting schedules to account for unexpected emergencies, data-driven decisions reduce downtime and improve overall operational flow.

Predictive Capabilities

Analytics does not just reveal what is happening—it forecasts what is likely to occur. Predictive algorithms analyze historical data to anticipate patient volumes, surgical demand, and resource needs. This foresight allows hospitals to prepare adequately, minimizing the risk of scheduling conflicts or last-minute cancellations. For instance, predictive scheduling tools can identify trends in surgeon availability and patient preferences, ensuring block utilization maximization without overburdening staff. A Midwest hospital implementing such tools saw a 25% reduction in underutilized OR blocks, improving patient access and financial performance.

Performance Monitoring

Maintaining long-term OR performance relies on ongoing evaluation, and data analytics offers a robust framework for monitoring key metrics over time. By tracking performance indicators such as turnover times, block utilization rates, and on-time starts for the first case, hospitals can identify areas for improvement and implement focused interventions. For instance, a perioperative team using analytics to assess adherence to scheduled start times discovered frequent delays in pre-surgical preparations. After addressing the underlying causes, they improved first-case on-time starts by 20%, resulting in better patient satisfaction and more predictable operations.

Broader Impacts on Accountability

Data analytics also fosters accountability by making performance visible at every level of the surgical team. Surgeons, nurses, and support staff can track their impact on OR performance, fostering a culture where everyone is committed to continuous improvement. For hospital administrators, analytics provides evidence-based insights, making it easier to justify resource allocation and strategic decisions. In the OR, where every second counts and inefficiencies can have significant consequences; data analytics is an essential tool for achieving operational excellence. Empowering leaders and teams with timely, accurate information bridges the gap between clinical priorities and operational goals, creating a high-performing surgical environment.

Key Applications of Data Analytics in the OR

Integrating data analytics into operating room (OR) workflows offers transformative potential across multiple dimensions. From scheduling optimization to infection control, analytics-driven insights empower healthcare teams to enhance efficiency, reduce costs, and improve patient outcomes. By understanding the key applications of data analytics, hospitals can unlock opportunities for sustained operational excellence.

Scheduling Optimization

Effective scheduling is critical for ensuring smooth OR operations. Analytics tools use predictive algorithms to align surgeon availability with patient demand, minimizing idle time and maximizing block utilization. For example, AI-powered platforms like Qventus or Epic's OR scheduling modules analyze historical patterns to forecast peak times, potential cancellations, and resource needs. A Midwest hospital reduced underutilized operating room time by 25% by implementing predictive scheduling tools, allowing it to perform more surgeries without adding extra operating rooms or staff. This optimization not only improved patient access but also boosted hospital revenue.

Turnover Time Reduction

Turnover times—the intervals between consecutive surgeries—are a crucial metric in OR efficiency. Analytics can identify bottlenecks in cleaning, equipment setup, or patient preparation, enabling targeted interventions. Through the analysis of time-motion data, one hospital identified that delays in room cleaning were responsible for 70% of turnover inefficiencies. By adopting a data-driven workflow, the hospital reduced turnover times by an average of 10 minutes per procedure, enabling an additional 200 surgeries per year and yielding substantial financial benefits.

Supply Chain Management

Surgical supplies are among the most significant expenses in the OR. Real-time analytics tools track inventory levels, usage patterns, and expiration dates, helping hospitals minimize waste and avoid stockouts.

For example, a hospital using data analytics discovered that certain high-cost implants were frequently expired or underutilized. By adjusting inventory policies and adopting just-in-time supply ordering, the hospital reduced waste by 30% and saved hundreds of thousands of dollars annually.

Performance Benchmarking

Comparing OR performance metrics across departments, facilities, or even against industry benchmarks allows hospitals to identify areas for improvement and replicate best practices. A multi-hospital system that implemented benchmarking software found that one of its locations had significantly lower turnover times due to a streamlined cleaning protocol.

Replicating this approach across all facilities led to a 10-minute reduction in average turnover times and improved operational consistency.

Infection Control

Data analytics is vital in monitoring trends in surgical site infections (SSIs) and identifying contributing factors. By correlating variables such as room temperature, instrument sterilization processes, and staff compliance with hand hygiene protocols, hospitals can implement targeted interventions to reduce infection rates. For instance, a teaching hospital used analytics to track SSI rates across procedures and found infections more likely in cases with longer turnover times. After addressing the issue, SSI rates decreased by 15%, improving patient outcomes and reducing readmission costs.

Bridging Insight and Action

The applications of data analytics in the OR go beyond theoretical possibilities—they deliver measurable improvements in day-to-day operations. Whether optimizing schedules, reducing waste, or improving patient safety, integrating data-driven insights ensures that hospitals operate at their highest potential. By leveraging these tools, healthcare teams can create an environment where efficiency and excellence coexist, benefiting patients and providers.

Challenges in Implementing Data Analytics

While the potential of data analytics in the OR is undeniable, the road to fully integrating these technologies is not without obstacles. Healthcare systems frequently encounter obstacles, ranging from technical constraints to organizational resistance, that must be overcome to fully unlock the potential of analytics-driven decision-making.

Data Integration

The fragmented nature of healthcare systems presents a significant hurdle to effective data analytics. Many hospitals operate with siloed data systems, including electronic health records (EHRs), scheduling platforms, and inventory management tools, which fail to communicate seamlessly. Without integration, valuable insights remain trapped within individual platforms, limiting their applicability to broader OR workflows. For example, a hospital may use one system to track OR schedules and another for patient outcomes, missing opportunities to connect how delays impact recovery times or satisfaction scores.

Solution: Investing in interoperable platforms or middleware solutions that aggregate and harmonize data across systems is critical. Hospitals like Johns Hopkins have adopted unified dashboards that pull data from multiple sources, creating a single source of truth for OR management. This integration reduces duplication, streamlines workflows, and enhances the reliability of analytics.

Data Quality

The adage "garbage in, garbage out" is particularly relevant in data analytics. Incomplete, inaccurate, or outdated data can lead to flawed analyses and misguided decisions. For instance, scheduling predictions based on incomplete historical data might result in overbooking or underutilized OR blocks.

Strategy: Implementing robust data governance practices is essential. These practices include regular audits, standardized data entry protocols, and automated quality checks to ensure the integrity of the information-feeding analytics platforms. Training staff to input accurate data and leveraging AI tools for anomaly detection can further enhance data quality.

Staff Resistance

Introducing data analytics tools often encounters pushback from OR teams unfamiliar with technology or skeptical about its benefits. Some staff may see analytics as an added burden rather than a solution, while others may fear excessive monitoring.

Approach: Comprehensive training programs and transparent communication about the value of analytics are vital. For example, demonstrating how real-time dashboards can alleviate scheduling conflicts or reduce idle time helps build trust and buy-in. Encouraging staff participation in selecting and implementing tools fosters a sense of ownership and reduces resistance.

Cost of Implementation

Adopting advanced analytics platforms can be a significant financial investment, particularly for smaller hospitals or those operating on tight budgets. Beyond purchasing software, costs often include hardware upgrades, staff training, and ongoing maintenance.

Solution: Hospitals should start with pilot programs to demonstrate return on investment (ROI) before committing to full-scale implementation. For example, a hospital in the Midwest piloted an AI-driven scheduling tool in three ORs, leading to a 20% increase in block utilization. The savings and additional revenue generated by the pilot justified the tool's expansion to all ORs.

Cultural and Organizational Challenges

Even when teams overcome technical barriers, embedding data analytics into the culture of OR operations can be challenging. Staff may be used to making decisions based on intuition or experience instead of data.

Action Plan: Leadership must champion the cultural shift toward data-driven decision-making. Regularly highlighting success stories—such as reduced turnover times or cost savings—demonstrates the tangible benefits of analytics. Engaging all levels of staff in discussions about analytics goals and progress ensures alignment and fosters a collaborative environment.

Overcoming the Barriers

Implementing data analytics in the OR is a complex but achievable goal. By addressing technical limitations, ensuring data accuracy, and fostering a supportive culture, hospitals can pave the way for analytics-driven excellence. The challenges, while significant, are far outweighed by the potential to revolutionize OR efficiency, improve patient outcomes, and drive financial performance. Hospitals that take a proactive, incremental approach to analytics adoption will position themselves as leaders in the future of healthcare innovation.

Case Study: Data-Driven OR Optimization

Real-world applications best illustrate the transformative potential of data analytics in operating rooms (ORs). This case study highlights how one regional hospital leveraged analytics to address inefficiencies and achieve measurable improvements in OR performance.

Situation: A regional hospital with eight ORs was struggling with operational inefficiencies. Turnover times consistently exceeded benchmarks, underutilized blocks were commonplace, and scheduling conflicts were causing delays. These issues disrupted surgical workflows and led to staff dissatisfaction, increased patient wait times, and lost revenue opportunities.

Task: Hospital leadership acknowledged the need for a comprehensive, data-driven strategy to tackle these inefficiencies. Their main objectives were to minimize turnover times, optimize OR utilization, and enhance staff and patient satisfaction.

Action: To tackle these challenges, the hospital implemented a multi-faceted analytics-driven strategy:

Real-Time Dashboards
The hospital adopted a real-time dashboard system to monitor key performance indicators (KPIs) such as turnover times, block utilization rates, and first-case on-time starts. This centralized platform provided the OR team with immediate visibility into ongoing operations, enabling faster identification and resolution of bottlenecks.

Data Analysis of Turnover Times

A detailed analysis of time-motion data revealed specific inefficiencies in cleaning and equipment preparation processes. For
instance, cleaning crews were frequently delayed because of poor
communication regarding surgery end times. The hospital significantly reduced idle times by implementing automated alerts to notify environmental services (EVS) teams when a procedure neared
completion.

Predictive Scheduling Tools

The hospital integrated predictive analytics software into its scheduling process. This tool used historical data to forecast demand and
allocate surgeon block time more effectively. The hospital identified
surgeons with frequent cancellations and adjusted their schedules
to optimize OR availability.

Staff Engagement and Training

The leadership trained staff on the new tools and promoted a data-driven mindset. They encouraged team members to provide
feedback, which they used to continuously improve the analytics
systems.

Result: The impact of these interventions was both immediate and significant:

- Turnover Times Reduced by 18%
- Streamlined workflows and improved coordination enabled
  the hospital to cut average turnover times by 18% within six
  months. This workflow translates to an additional 1,200 minutes of available OR time each month.
- OR Utilization Increased by 12%
- Predictive scheduling and better block allocation led to more
  efficient use of available OR time, and the hospital saw a notice-
  able uptick in the number of weekly surgeries.

- Revenue Growth of $1.2 Million Annually
- The additional surgical cases facilitated by optimized OR utilization resulted in a revenue increase of $1.2 million annually.
- Improved Staff Satisfaction
- Predictable schedules and reduced delays boosted morale among OR staff, with post-implementation surveys showing a 25% improvement in job satisfaction.

Lessons Learned

This case study underscores the importance of a comprehensive approach to data-driven OR optimization.

Key takeaways include:

- The Power of Visibility: Real-time dashboards empower teams to take proactive action, ensuring smoother operations.
- Targeted Interventions Matter: Data analytics can pinpoint specific inefficiencies, allowing hospitals to focus their efforts where they will have the most impact.
- Engagement Drives Success: Actively involving staff in the implementation process fosters buy-in and ensures long-term sustainability.

This example demonstrates that data analytics is not just a tool for monitoring OR performance but a strategic transformation enabler. Hospitals that invest in analytics-driven solutions can achieve measurable improvements in efficiency, financial performance, and team satisfaction.

Tools for OR Data Analytics: Unlocking Potential Briefly

Data analytics tools have revolutionized operating rooms (ORs), providing actionable insights to enhance efficiency and outcomes. These tools are the backbone for decision-making and continuous improvement in OR environments.

Real-Time Dashboards: Platforms like Tableau or Qventus visualize critical metrics like turnover times and block utilization, empowering teams with immediate insights to address bottlenecks.

AI-Powered Scheduling: Advanced tools like Epic and Cerner optimize OR schedules by aligning surgeon availability with patient needs, reducing underutilized blocks.

Predictive Analytics Platforms: These systems forecast trends in surgical demand, enabling better preparation and resource allocation and directly reducing cancellations.

Benchmarking Software: Multi-hospital systems leverage these tools to compare performance metrics and implement best practices, driving systemwide improvements.

When integrated effectively, these tools transform data into actionable strategies, fostering operational excellence while minimizing inefficiencies.

Conclusion: Harnessing the Power of Data for OR Excellence

Data analytics has become an essential tool for improving efficiency, enhancing patient outcomes, and achieving operational excellence in the operating room. By transforming raw data into actionable insights, healthcare organizations can tackle inefficiencies, optimize scheduling, and maximize resource utilization, all while upholding the highest standards of patient care.

This chapter has examined how real-time dashboards, AI-powered scheduling, and predictive analytics are revolutionizing OR operations. These technologies help reduce turnover times, streamline workflows, and enable leaders to make data-driven decisions that balance cost control with quality care. The use of benchmarking software further ensures that best practices are identified and consistently applied across facilities, promoting a culture of continuous improvement.

As the healthcare landscape continues to evolve, the role of data analytics will expand, with advancements in AI, IoT, and personalized surgery set to reshape the future of OR operations. Hospitals that adopt these technologies and overcome challenges related to data integration, accuracy, and adoption will position themselves as leaders in both surgical innovation and patient care.

In the next chapter, we explore how emerging trends and innovations are shaping the future of the OR, building on the foundational principles discussed here to elevate efficiency and excellence to new levels.

CHAPTER 10

INNOVATION AND EMERGING TRENDS IN OR EFFICIENCY
Revolutionizing Surgical Care with Technology

Introduction

The operating room (OR) is a dynamic arena where technology, innovation, and human expertise intersect to deliver life-saving care. Over the years, advancements in robotics, artificial intelligence (AI), and augmented reality (AR) have transformed how surgeries are performed and managed. Beyond adopting new tools, broader trends like sustainability and precision medicine are reshaping the OR landscape, paving the way for more efficient, patient-centered care.

In this chapter, we examine the innovations driving OR proficiency, from cutting-edge surgical systems to eco-friendly practices, and delve into the trends shaping the future of surgical care. With a greater understanding of the challenges and strategies for integrating these advancements; healthcare leaders and surgical teams can prepare to navigate the ever-evolving healthcare environment while delivering exceptional patient outcomes.

The Role of Innovation in OR Efficiency

Innovation is a cornerstone of transformation in the operating room (OR), where integrating advanced tools, technologies, and processes continues redefining operational and clinical excellence. Beyond improving surgical precision and patient outcomes, innovation addresses inefficiencies, enhances team collaboration, and sets the stage for the future of healthcare. Understanding the multi-faceted role of innovation in OR performance requires a closer examination of how technology and methodology converge to create sustainable improvements.

Driving Technology-Enabled Improvements

The advent of innovative technologies has revolutionized OR workflows. Robotic surgery platforms, artificial intelligence (AI), and augmented reality (AR) are more than just tools—they change thinking about how surgeries are performed and managed. For instance, robotic-assisted systems offer unparalleled precision, reducing complications and recovery times, while AI-driven scheduling tools analyze historical data to optimize block utilization and prevent delays. Integrating such technologies streamlines surgical procedures, minimizes downtime, and enables healthcare teams to operate with heightened accuracy and confidence.

Optimizing Processes with Innovation

Innovation is not confined to technology alone but extends to rethinking processes. When applied in the OR, Lean and Six Sigma eliminate waste, standardize workflows, and enhance resource allocation. Hospitals that embrace these methodologies report measurable gains, such as reduced turnover times and improved utilization rates. These process-driven innovations ensure that every minute and every tool in the OR contributes meaningfully to operations without compromising patient safety.

Fostering a Collaborative Ecosystem

Innovation promotes a collaborative environment where interdisciplinary teams function seamlessly. Emerging platforms facilitate real-time communication and data sharing, ensuring surgeons, anesthesiologists, nurses, and technicians stay aligned at every step. These collaborative ecosystems reduce redundancies, mitigate errors, and strengthen accountability, leading to smoother surgical operations. The constructive collaboration created through these innovations enhances performance, staff morale, and patient trust.

A Catalyst for Continuous Improvement

The role of innovation is not static; it evolves alongside advancements in science and technology. Continuous improvement is at the heart of innovation in the OR, with hospitals leveraging analytics to measure the impact of new tools and methodologies. By iterating on successful strategies and adopting adaptive technologies, healthcare organizations can maintain a trajectory of progress, ensuring that their ORs remain at the forefront of operational and clinical efficiency.

Innovation serves as both a driver and enabler of OR optimization. Whether through the adoption of groundbreaking technologies or the refinement of existing workflows, the commitment to innovation transforms the OR into a hub of excellence. It bridges the gap between current capabilities and future possibilities, preparing healthcare institutions to meet the demands of an evolving landscape.

Emerging Technologies in the OR

The operating room (OR) is at the forefront of technological evolution, where emerging innovations continuously redefine surgical capabilities and operational workflows. These technologies address long-standing inefficiencies, elevate surgical precision, and improve patient outcomes. As these advancements integrate into OR environments, they transform the standards of modern surgical care.

Robotic-Assisted Surgery: Revolutionizing Precision

Robotic-assisted systems have transformed surgeries, offering surgeons enhanced dexterity and control. Platforms such as robotic arms enable minimally invasive procedures with precision beyond the capability of human hands. This technology not only shortens patient recovery times, but decreases complication rates, leading to improved outcomes.

Advantages include:

- Smaller incisions lead to faster healing.
- Greater accuracy in complex procedures, such as urologic and cardiac surgeries.
- Enhanced surgeon ergonomics, reducing fatigue during lengthy operations.

Artificial Intelligence (AI): Enhancing Decision-Making

AI's role in the OR extends beyond scheduling; it has become a critical tool in predicting surgical outcomes, optimizing workflows, and ensuring resource allocation. By analyzing large datasets, AI-driven systems can forecast patient-specific complications and recommend tailored interventions. For example: AI algorithms help predict case durations, ensuring efficient scheduling and better block utilization. Machine learning tools assist in identifying anomalies during procedures and support clinical decisions in real-time.

Augmented Reality (AR) and Virtual Reality (VR): Expanding Surgical Visualization

AR and VR have opened new dimensions in pre-operative planning, intraoperative guidance, and surgeon training. AR overlays critical anatomical information in the surgical field, enhancing a surgeon's ability to navigate complex structures. Meanwhile, VR creates immersive simulations for surgical practice, allowing teams to perfect techniques in a risk-free environment.

Key applications include:
- AR-guided orthopedic and neurosurgical procedures for precise alignment and placement.
- VR-based training programs allow surgeons to refine their skills before performing real-world operations.
- 3D Printing: Personalized Surgical Tools
- 3D printing technology is bridging the gap between patient-specific needs and surgical solutions. Hospitals now use 3D-printed anatomical models for pre-operative planning and custom implants for unique cases.

Key benefits:
- Patient-specific implants reduce the risk of complications and enhance surgical fit.
- Anatomical models improve surgical team comprehension of complex cases.
- Wearable Technology: Monitoring and Enhancing Performance

Wearables designed for OR staff track physiological metrics such as fatigue, stress levels, and posture during procedures. This data helps optimize staff well-being, indirectly contributing to surgical efficiency and safety.

Impact areas:
- Providing real-time feedback on ergonomics to prevent strain and improve precision.
- Supporting surgeon endurance during prolonged procedures.

Integrated Systems: A Holistic Approach
Emerging technologies are increasingly interconnected, creating smarter ORs where data flows seamlessly between tools, teams, and systems.

For example:
- Integration of AI with robotic systems enables predictive interventions.
- Smart sensors track and automate equipment readiness, reducing delays.

In summary, emerging technologies are expanding surgical capabilities and ushering in a more efficient, patient-focused operating room. By adopting these innovations, healthcare organizations can significantly enhance operational performance and clinical outcomes, positioning themselves as leaders in the evolving healthcare landscape.

Trends Shaping the Future of OR Efficiency

As the healthcare landscape evolves, broader trends are shaping the future of OR productivity. These trends go beyond individual technologies, integrating systemic changes that align surgical practices with contemporary demands for quality, sustainability, and patient-centered care. Understanding these trends offers hospitals a roadmap for staying competitive and meeting the needs of an increasingly informed patient population.

Precision Medicine: Tailoring Surgical Care

Precision medicine focuses on individualized treatment plans based on genetic, molecular, and environmental factors. In the OR, this approach allows for better patient selection, tailored surgical techniques, and optimized outcomes.

Impact on Surgery: By integrating patient-specific data, surgeons can choose the most appropriate interventions, minimizing complications and improving recovery times.

Example: Personalized implants and targeted therapies have already begun to reduce variability in outcomes for orthopedic and oncologic procedures.

Sustainability in Healthcare

With increasing awareness of environmental impacts, ORs are adopting sustainable practices to reduce waste and energy consumption while maintaining safety and efficiency.

Eco-Friendly Practices: Hospitals are switching to reusable surgical instruments and implementing energy-efficient OR systems.

Financial Benefits: Sustainable practices benefit the environment and reduce operational costs. For instance, managing surgical waste more effectively has led to significant cost savings for hospitals globally.

Value-Based Care Models

Value-based care prioritizes quality and cost-effectiveness over volume. OR efficiency initiatives are crucial in meeting these goals, ensuring surgeries are timely, cost-efficient, and focused on optimal outcomes.

Enhanced Metrics: Key performance indicators, such as patient satisfaction, surgical outcomes, and readmission rates, directly impact value-based care.

Impact: Aligning OR practices with value-based models enhances hospital reimbursement rates and builds trust with payers and patients.

Integrated Care Pathways

An integrated approach across pre-operative, intraoperative, and postoperative phases ensures a seamless surgical journey for patients.

Benefits: Patients experience fewer delays, better communication with care teams, and improved recovery times.

Example: Hospitals using integrated care pathways have reported higher patient satisfaction scores and reduced lengths of stay.

Patient-Centered Innovations
Emerging innovations, such as telemedicine and remote monitoring, have expanded the OR's reach beyond the surgical suite. These tools improve pre-operative preparation and postoperative follow-up, enhancing patient experience.

Telemedicine Applications: Virtual consultations streamline pre-surgical evaluations, reducing no-shows and cancellations.
Remote Monitoring: Postoperative tools enable real-time tracking of recovery, helping surgeons address complications early and improve outcomes.

Conclusion

Innovation and emerging trends are revolutionizing the operating room, creating opportunities for hospitals to deliver safer, faster, and more cost-effective surgical care. By embracing these advancements, healthcare organizations can address inefficiencies, enhance clinical outcomes, and improve patient satisfaction.

However, the path forward requires a thoughtful balance between adoption and implementation. Leaders must assess the relevance of these trends to their specific organizational needs, ensuring that modern technologies align with operational goals and patient care standards. Training and stakeholder engagement will be critical in overcoming barriers such as resistance to change and financial constraints.

Ultimately, the successful integration of innovation into the OR environment represents a commitment to excellence in surgical care. By staying ahead of emerging trends, hospitals can solidify their reputation as pioneers in modern medicine, driving better outcomes for patients, staff, and the broader healthcare ecosystem. As the concluding chapter approaches, we will reflect on the key insights from this book and outline actionable steps for achieving and sustaining excellence in the OR.

CHAPTER 11

SYSTEMWIDE LEADERSHIP IN OPERATING ROOM MANAGEMENT
Unifying Strategy, Efficiency, and Collaboration

Introduction

Operating room (OR) management extends beyond individual facilities; it is a systemwide endeavor requiring unified leadership, cohesive strategies, and cross-functional collaboration. As healthcare systems grow larger and more complex, the role of systemwide leadership in OR management has never been more critical. Centralizing OR operations can enhance resource allocation, boost productivity, and maintain consistency in patient care. However, to achieve these goals, it is crucial to strike a balance between broad policies and the need for local flexibility, as each facility encounters its own distinct challenges.

This chapter discusses the principles of systemwide OR leadership, highlighting its role in standardizing practices, leveraging data-driven strategies, and fostering a culture of accountability across multiple facilities. It also examines real-world applications and offers actionable insights for leaders aiming to maximize efficiency and outcomes within large healthcare networks. Systemwide OR management demands more than strategic oversight—it requires empowering facility leaders, aligning goals with systemwide objectives, and embracing innovation to ensure operational and clinical excellence.

Setting a Unified Vision for Systemwide OR Management

A unified vision serves as the compass guiding systemwide OR management. It ensures that all facilities, regardless of size or specialty, align with the health system's overarching goals. In an environment as complex as healthcare, where inefficiencies can ripple across an entire network, a shared vision is essential for achieving consistent outcomes and operational excellence.

Why a Unified Vision Matters

A clear, systemwide vision reduces variability and provides a roadmap for every facility to contribute toward common objectives. This vision often includes optimizing OR utilization, improving patient safety, and standardizing turnover procedures across all facilities. For example, a health system might set ambitious yet achievable goals such as increasing OR utilization to over 85% and reducing surgical cancellations by 20%.

However, this vision must go beyond aspirational, requiring clear, actionable steps to become a reality. Engaging stakeholders, including surgeons, administrators, and frontline OR staff, is essential. These teams offer valuable insights that shape objectives and promote buy-in. Ongoing communication through leadership forums, team meetings, and regular updates helps ensure the vision remains shared and sustained. Establishing a unified vision; healthcare systems can create a shared sense of purpose that empowers teams across facilities to deliver high-quality, efficient care. This foundation enables the alignment of daily operations with long-term strategic goals.

Developing Systemwide Objectives and Scorecards
Creating Clear Metrics for Success

Establishing measurable objectives is the next step in operationalizing a unified vision. Systemwide objectives act as benchmarks to gauge success across facilities. Metrics like OR utilization, turnover times, and cost per case offer quantifiable insights into performance, making it easier to identify strengths and areas for improvement.

For example, a scorecard might track metrics such as:

- OR Utilization: Targeting 85% or higher to maximize efficiency.
- Turnover Time: Maintaining an average of fewer than 25 minutes between cases.
- First-Case On-Time Starts: Ensuring over 90% punctuality to avoid cascading delays.

Building a Systemwide Scorecard

A systemwide scorecard consolidates data from all facilities, offering a comprehensive view of performance. This transparency promotes accountability and fosters competition in a healthy, constructive way. For instance, a scorecard that monitors monthly OR utilization and quarterly turnover times can highlight facilities excelling in these areas and serve as a model for others to emulate.

Scorecards also align leadership teams by providing a shared reference point during performance reviews, strategic planning sessions, and governance meetings. This alignment ensures that every facility remains on track toward systemwide goals.

Standardizing Processes Across Facilities
Consistency as a Cornerstone of Efficiency
Standardization is key to achieving predictable, high-quality outcomes across a health system. By minimizing variability in workflows, hospitals can reduce inefficiencies, streamline operations, and enhance patient safety. Key areas for standardization include

surgical preference cards, scheduling protocols, and turnover procedures. For instance, a uniform process for updating preference cards ensures surgeons across all facilities have the necessary tools and supplies without delay. Similarly, centralized scheduling protocols enable efficient resource allocation by prioritizing high-demand cases and reducing idle OR time.

Turnover procedures offer another opportunity for standardization. Facilities can adopt consistent cleaning and setup protocols, ensuring all teams follow best practices to minimize downtime between cases. This approach seamlessly transitions across different facilities, improving overall system performance.

Standardizing Equipment Across Facilities

Standardizing equipment across multiple facilities is essential for effective systemwide OR management. It lowers costs, simplifies training, and supports consistent patient outcomes. Although individual facilities may have specific needs, aligning equipment standards provides a solid foundation for operational consistency and long-term growth.

The Benefits of Standardization

Cost Efficiency

Purchasing equipment in bulk for multiple facilities often leads to significant cost savings through vendor negotiations and bulk discounts. Additionally, standardized equipment reduces maintenance costs by enabling uniform servicing contracts and minimizing the need for specialized spare parts.

Example: A health system reduced equipment procurement costs by 15% after consolidating purchasing agreements across its network.

Streamlined Training

Standardizing training programs across facilities that use the same equipment makes onboarding and skill development more efficient. This approach ensures that staff from different locations can easily support each other when needed, fostering a more versatile workforce.

Consistent Patient Care

Standardized tools ensure surgical teams across facilities have access to the same equipment quality, reducing outcome variability. Surgeons can rely on familiar tools, improving confidence and precision during procedures.

Overcoming Challenges in Standardization

Facility-Specific Needs

Not all facilities need the same equipment sophistication, as case complexity and patient demographics vary. To address this, leadership should identify core equipment to standardize while allowing specialized tools in specific settings.

Approach: Conduct a needs assessment across facilities to determine which equipment aligns with shared goals and which may need localized customization.

Staff Adaptation

Transitioning to standardized equipment can be challenging for staff accustomed to different tools. Hands-on training and emphasizing the benefits of standardization—such as improved efficiency and reduced downtime—can mitigate this challenge.

Vendor Partnerships

Establishing systemwide contracts with vendors can sometimes limit flexibility for individual facilities. Leaders should negotiate agreements that balance cost savings with the ability to meet specific facility requirements.

Building a Systemwide Standardization Framework

Centralized Procurement

Create a centralized committee to oversee equipment selection and purchasing. This committee would ensure alignment with systemwide goals while incorporating input from clinical staff.

Data-Driven Decisions

Use data analytics to evaluate equipment utilization, maintenance costs, and facility performance. This analysis helps identify the most cost-effective and reliable tools for standardization.

Pilot Programs

Implement standardization on a smaller scale before expanding systemwide. This standardization allows testing and refinement while building staff confidence in the initiative. Standardizing equipment across facilities is a logistical effort and a strategic initiative aligning operational goals with patient-centered care. By fostering collaboration and leveraging systemwide resources, healthcare organizations can unlock efficiency gains and deliver consistent outcomes across their networks.

Data Integration for Systemwide Insights

Data integration is the cornerstone of achieving systemwide optimization in OR management. Hospitals generate vast amounts of data from scheduling systems, electronic health records (EHRs), supply chains, and financial operations. Effectively consolidating and analyzing this data allows leaders to identify trends, optimize workflows, and make informed decisions.

Why It Matters: Integrated data systems provide a unified view of OR performance across facilities, highlighting areas for improvement and standardization. For example, comparing block utilization rates across facilities can reveal disparities from scheduling inefficiencies or equipment availability.

Key Considerations:
- Interoperability: Invest in platforms that seamlessly connect various data sources.
- Predictive Analytics: Use historical data to forecast surgical demand, helping to allocate resources proactively.
- Data Governance: Establish protocols to ensure data accuracy and security.

Data-driven decision-making enables leaders to create targeted strategies that improve operations while ensuring the delivery of high-quality patient care.

Governance and Leadership for Systemwide OR Management

Leadership plays a pivotal role in the success of systemwide OR management, yet the choice of who leads this effort significantly impacts its effectiveness. Traditionally, surgeons or nurses have held leadership roles due to their clinical expertise. However, a change in thinking is needed to appoint leaders with operational, business, and financial acumen who can think beyond the clinical aspects and bring a process-oriented approach to OR management.

Why Governance Matters: Effective governance ensures accountability, consistency, and alignment across all facilities in a health system. Without a strong governance framework, individual facilities may operate in silos, leading to inefficiencies and fragmented care.

The Ideal OR Leader: While clinical expertise is essential, system-wide OR leadership demands a distinct skill set. Leaders with solid operational and financial experience can offer a fresh perspective on long-standing challenges, emphasizing effectiveness, resource management, and sustainability.

How to Advocate for Change:
- Emphasize Collaborative Leadership: Highlight the need for leaders who can unify clinical and administrative teams.
- Present Outcomes: Data can demonstrate how process-oriented leadership drives measurable improvements in OR efficiency and financial performance.
- Build Political Consensus: Frame the conversation around enhancing patient care and operational sustainability, avoiding language that may dismiss clinical leaders' contributions.

By selecting leaders with diverse skill sets and fostering a culture of collaboration, healthcare systems can achieve operational excellence without losing sight of their mission to deliver exceptional patient care.

Addressing Challenges in Systemwide OR Management
- Staffing and Resource Allocation: Develop float pools and centralized staffing models to manage shortages.
- Financial Constraints: Balance budgets across facilities while ensuring quality care.
- Cultural Resistance: Engage teams early in the change process to gain buy-in and minimize resistance.

Case Study: Systemwide OR Management Success

Situation: A 15-hospital health system faced inconsistent OR utilization, with smaller facilities underperforming and larger ones overburdened.

Task: Develop a unified systemwide strategy to improve efficiency and balance workloads.

Action:
1. Standardized scheduling and turnover protocols across all facilities.
2. Implementation of a centralized dashboard for tracking systemwide performance.
3. Standardized equipment lists high-volume procedures to streamline operations.

Result:
- OR utilization increased by 12% systemwide.
- Annual cost savings of $4.5 million through equipment standardization and better resource allocation.
- Improved staff satisfaction scores across facilities.

The Future of Systemwide OR Leadership
- **Innovation:** Incorporate innovative OR technologies and robotics across facilities and use advanced analytics to further optimize workflows.
- **Patient-Centered Care:** Align system goals with patient outcomes to ensure high-quality care.
- **Continuous Improvement:** Regularly review and update strategies to adapt to new challenges and opportunities.

Conclusion

Managing ORs across a health system is a complex but achievable task when leaders align vision, standardize processes, and leverage data-driven insights. By including equipment standardization and other systemwide strategies, health systems can achieve operational excellence, financial sustainability, and improved patient outcomes.

CHAPTER 12

SUSTAINING EXCELLENCE IN THE OPERATING ROOM

Introduction

Achieving success in the operating room (OR) is important, but maintaining it over time requires constant effort and adaptation. Sustaining excellence in the OR is not a one-time goal; it is an ongoing journey that requires aligning processes, technology, and personnel with the ever-changing needs of healthcare.

This chapter synthesizes the insights from previous chapters and focuses on actionable strategies to ensure long-term success. By fostering a culture of continuous improvement, leveraging data-driven insights, and empowering teams, hospitals can sustain operational excellence and adapt to future challenges.

The Pillars of Sustained OR Excellence

Long-term efficiency in the OR relies on three core pillars:

Culture of Continuous Improvement:
- Encourage a mindset where teams consistently seek ways to improve workflows.

Example: A hospital conducting quarterly performance audits uncovered opportunities to save $500,000 each year.

Strong Leadership:
- Leaders play a crucial role in setting expectations, providing resources, and maintaining accountability.

Strategy: Regular leadership rounds in the OR to observe workflows and gather staff input.

Technological Integration:
- Seamless integration of technology ensures that innovations remain relevant and impactful.

Case Study: A hospital upgraded its scheduling software every two years, maintaining a 90% block utilization rate.

Strategies for Sustaining Efficiency

To build and maintain OR excellence, hospitals must adopt strategies that focus on consistency and adaptability:

Ongoing Training and Development:
- Regularly update staff on new tools, protocols, and best practices.

Approach: Incorporate simulation-based training to enhance team collaboration and technical skills.

Standardization with Flexibility:
- Standardize processes to reduce variability while allowing customization based on specific cases.

Example: Use checklists for all procedures but adjust for complex surgeries as needed.

Periodic Performance Reviews:
- Conduct reviews to measure progress, address bottlenecks, and recalibrate goals.

Tools: Use data dashboards to track turnover times, utilization rates, and cost per case.

Proactive Maintenance of Equipment:
- Regular maintenance schedules prevent unexpected downtimes and delays.

Impact: Increased reliability of surgical tools and technology reduces case cancellations.

Overcoming Challenges in Sustaining Excellence

Even well-functioning ORs face challenges in maintaining efficiency.

Common obstacles include:

- Staff Turnover: Frequent staff changes disrupt established workflows and require additional training.

Solution: Develop robust onboarding programs and mentorship initiatives.

- Technological Obsolescence: Rapid advancements in technology can render current systems outdated.

Strategy: Establish a technology roadmap to plan upgrades and replacements.

- Complacency: Teams may grow complacent after achieving initial efficiency gains.

Approach: Set incremental improvement goals to keep teams engaged and motivated.

- External Factors: Changes in regulations, reimbursement models, or patient demographics can impact operations.

Action Plan: Stay informed about industry trends and adjust strategies accordingly.

Case Study: A Blueprint for Sustained OR Excellence

Situation: A 10-OR suburban hospital achieved significant efficiency improvements but struggled to maintain these gains over time.

Task: Develop a sustainable framework to ensure consistent OR performance.

Action:
1. Implemented a quarterly review process to track key performance indicators (KPIs) and gather staff feedback.
2. Created a cross-disciplinary task force to address emerging challenges and recommend solutions.
3. Established a recognition program to celebrate teams that consistently met efficiency targets.

Result:
- Turnover times remained stable at 22 minutes, even with staff turnover.
- Patient satisfaction scores increased by 15% over two years.
- The hospital maintained a 92% block utilization rate, generating an additional $1.8 million annually.

Key Performance Indicators for Sustained Success

Hospitals must monitor specific KPIs to ensure that OR operations remain efficient and effective.

Here are a few examples:

Operational Metrics:

- Turnover Time: Maintain consistency across all ORs.
- First-Case On-Time Starts: Aim for at least 90% adherence.

Financial Metrics:

- Cost per Case: Track trends to identify areas for cost optimization.
- Revenue per OR Hour: Monitor the financial impact of efficiency initiatives.

Quality Metrics:

- Surgical Site Infections (SSIs): Focus on minimizing infections through enhanced protocols.
- Patient Satisfaction: Conduct surveys to assess the quality of care and movement areas for improvement.

Staff Metrics:

- Retention Rates: High retention indicates a positive work environment and stable teams.
- Engagement Scores: Measure staff morale and involvement in efficiency initiatives.

Building Resilience for the Future

Sustaining OR excellence also involves preparing for future challenges and opportunities.

Here are some examples:

- **Adapting to Regulatory Changes:** Stay proactive in meeting new compliance requirements, such as those related to value-based care.
- **Embracing Innovation:** Continuously explore emerging technologies and trends, such as smart ORs and autonomous robotics.
- **Focusing on Patient-Centered Care:** Incorporate patient feedback into efficiency initiatives to align operations with their needs and expectations.
- **Developing Future Leaders:** Invest in leadership development programs to ensure a pipeline of capable OR leaders.

Conclusion

Sustaining excellence in the OR is an ongoing process that requires commitment, collaboration, and adaptability. By building on the strategies and insights outlined in this book, hospitals can maintain high performance, deliver exceptional patient care, and confidently navigate the evolving healthcare confidence. The OR is a cornerstone of hospital success, and sustained excellence ensures it remains a beacon of innovation, efficiency, and quality.

CLOSING

A VISION FOR THE FUTURE OF OPERATING ROOMS

As we close this book, we must remember that the ultimate goal behind every effort, innovation, and strategy in the operating room (OR) is the patient. The OR transforms lives and restores health. In every decision we make, we must remain grounded in the singular question:

"How am I helping the patient by doing this? How am I making their life better and easier?"

This mindset ensures that our work connects to a higher purpose: serving the community. By putting the patient at the center of all we do, we elevate the quality of care, strengthen our commitment to safety and efficiency, and reinforce the humanity of healthcare.

A Call to Action

Let this principle guide your efforts as you apply the insights from this book to your OR:

1. For Leaders:
- Ask how your policies, investments, and strategies improve patient outcomes and experience.
- Inspire your teams to see the impact of their work beyond metrics—on the lives they touch daily.

2. For Perioperative Teams:
- In the high-pressure environment of the OR, remember that each step you take contributes to the patient's journey toward healing.
- Work with purpose, knowing that your precision and dedication directly impact lives.

3. For Future Professionals:
- Approach healthcare as more than a career—see it as a calling to serve and improve the lives of patients and communities.
- Let the question, "How am I helping the patient?" guide your growth and decisions.

A Vision for the Future

The future of the OR holds countless opportunities for innovation and improvement. Yet, the core of our work should always center on serving the patient. Whether through advancements in robotics, data analytics, or collaborative processes, our guiding principle must remain constant: the patient comes first.

This focus will drive operational excellence and uphold healthcare's profound mission of healing, serving, and enhancing lives.

This book serves as both a reminder and a guide to keeping you grounded in this higher purpose as you shape the future of surgical care and healthcare delivery.

BONUS INSIGHTS

Practical Applications:
Real-World Case Studies & Tools

Case Study 1: Reducing Day-of-Surgery Cancellations in a Health System

Background: A regional health system with a multi-facility setup identified a recurring issue: Day-of-Surgery (DOS) cancellations accounted for 41% of all surgical cancellations systemwide, significantly disrupting operations and impacting financial outcomes. On average, DOS cancellations affected 3.7% of total scheduled surgeries, posing operational challenges and reducing patient satisfaction. These cancellations caused last-minute schedule adjustments, underutilized operating rooms, and revenue losses. The system lacked accurate data to effectively understand and address the root causes of cancellations.

Objective - Health system launched a strategic initative to:
1. Reduce DOS cancellations.
2. Improve operational efficiency.
3. Enhance patient satisfaction.
4. Increase overall surgical case volumes.

Problem Definition: A multidisciplinary team, including perioperative directors, informatics specialists, clinical educators, and a surgeon champion, took the following steps:

- *Defined Cancellation Metrics:* Standardizing the definition of DOS cancellations to ensure consistency across all facilities.
- *Aligned with Policy:* Developing measures aligned with organizational policies to classify and assess cancellations accurately.
- *Streamlined Data Collection:* Reducing the number of cancellation categories from 50 to 20 to improve clarity and enable more meaningful analysis.

Root Cause Analysis: Through data analysis and stakeholder feedback, the team identified the following primary causes of DOS cancellations:

- *Pre-Procedural Testing Issues:* Numerous cancellations occurred due to incomplete or abnormal test results.
- *Non-Compliance with Pre-Operative Instructions:* Patients frequently failed to adhere to dietary restrictions, medication guidelines, or fasting protocols.
- *Patient-Related Factors:* Pre-operative testing revealed health issues such as elevated blood pressure, unmanaged diabetes, and other conditions.

Implementation of Solutions: To address these issues, the team deployed a comprehensive strategy:

Predictive Analytics:
- Developed a predictive model to identify patients at higher risk of cancellation 48 hours before surgery.
- Proactively contacted high-risk patients and their surgeons' offices to address potential issues in advance.

Standardized Communication:
- Conducted day-before-surgery phone calls to remind patients of fasting rules, medication schedules, and other pre-operative requirements.
- Introduced patient education programs on managing chronic conditions like diabetes and hypertension pre-surgery.

Optimized Scheduling:
- Reallocated surgeries with a high likelihood of cancellation to non-peak hours or designated operating rooms, minimizing disruption.
- Developed a protocol to schedule complex cases with a higher probability of cancellation in dedicated time slots.

Outcomes

Quantitative Results:
- Reduction in Cancellations: DOS cancellations decreased from 3.7% to 2.5% within six months of implementation.
- Improved Pre-Procedural Compliance: Patient adherence to pre-operative instructions increased by 25%.
- Increased OR Utilization: Operating room utilization improved by 12%, generating an estimated additional annual revenue of $1.5 million.

Operational Improvements
- *Streamlined Processes:* Simplifying and standardizing cancellation reporting processes across facilities.
- *Enhanced Patient Preparedness:* Patients better understood pre-operative requirements, reducing non-clinical cancellations.
- *Optimized Resources:* The team rescheduled high-risk cases efficiently, minimizing the impact on daily workflows.

Patient Satisfaction
- *Survey Scores:* Patient satisfaction scores related to surgical experiences increased by 18%.
- *Feedback:* Patients appreciated the proactive communication and educational efforts, leading to better-prepared surgeries.

Key Learnings
Importance of Data-Driven Decision Making
Predictive analytics proved instrumental in identifying at-risk cases and enabling proactive interventions.

- **Interdisciplinary Collaboration:** The involvement of perioperative leaders, clinicians, and administrative staff ensured the program's success by comprehensively addressing all facets of the issue.
- **Education as a Cornerstone:** Educating patients about pre-operative protocols significantly reduced non-compliance-related cancellations.
- **Flexible Scheduling:** Adopting a dynamic scheduling strategy mitigated the impact of inevitable cancellations on overall operations.

Replicability and Scalability
The success of this initiative provides a blueprint for other health systems facing similar challenges. Hospitals can replicate and scale this model across diverse settings by focusing on data standardization, proactive patient engagement, and operational adjustments.

Conclusion
This case study demonstrates the transformative potential of structured problem-solving, data analytics, and patient-centric strategies in reducing DOS cancellations. By addressing root causes and implementing targeted solutions, healthcare organizations can achieve operational excellence while enhancing patient outcomes and satisfaction.

Case Study 2: Surgical Preference Card Optimization in a Large Health System

Background: A regional health system faced significant inefficiencies in managing surgical preference cards, critical for ensuring that operating rooms (ORs) have the appropriate equipment and supplies for each procedure. Challenges included inconsistencies in preference card updates, significant waste of unused items, and high levels of non-value-added work for perioperative staff. Staff spent 60–80 hours per week returning and restocking unused supplies, which led to frustration, operational inefficiencies, and increased costs. The team needed a sustainable solution to streamline preference card management, reduce waste, and improve OR efficiency.

Impacts of Preference Cards on Various Touchpoints

Objective(s)
1. To create a standardized, systemwide process for preference card management.
2. To reduce the waste associated with unused supplies.
3. Improve collaboration and communication between clinical teams, service line managers, and supply chain staff.

Problem Identification - A multidisciplinary team conducted an initial assessment, identifying the following key challenges:

- *Inconsistent Processes:* Each facility had its manual, paper-based process for updating preference cards, leading to errors and inefficiencies.
- *High Waste Levels:* Over 120 items were routinely picked up for OR carts but often went unused and had to be restocked, creating an additional workload.

- *Communication Gaps:* Lack of structured communication between surgeons, OR staff, and Central Sterile Processing Department (CSPD) teams resulted in discrepancies and errors.

Data Analysis - The team analyzed preference card utilization data across two pilot locations, identifying the top 10% of highest-use cards for targeted improvements.

Key findings included:
- A high volume of redundant or outdated items on preference cards.
- Significant variability in how changes were communicated and implemented.
- Incidents related to missing or incorrect instruments contribute to delays.

Pilot Implementation - The initiative was piloted at two facilities, focusing on the following strategies:

Standardization of Processes:
- Developed a uniform process for updating preference cards, including a six-month review cycle with active surgeon participation.
- Introduced electronic documentation to replace manual updates, reducing human error.

Accomplishments:

Waste Reduction:
- Reviewed and streamlined preference cards by removing redundant items.
- Limited OR cart inventory is available for only high-use, essential supplies.

Enhanced Communication:

- Developed a clear workflow for surgeons to communicate preference card changes through OR nurses, who then relayed updates to clinical managers.
- Established a feedback loop to ensure updates were implemented and validated.

Technology Utilization:

- Used existing OR IT systems to track preference card usage and monitor waste metrics.
- Integrated data analytics to identify further opportunities for optimization.

Outcomes

Quantitative Results

- **Reduction in Non-Value-Added Work:** The time spent restocking unused items decreased by 45%, saving approximately 36 hours per week.
- **Waste Reduction:** The number of unused items on OR carts dropped by 30%.
- **Efficiency Gains:** Preference card updates became 25% faster due to standardized processes and electronic documentation.

Operational Improvements

- *Consistency Across Facilities:* Standardized processes reduced variability in preference card management, improving reliability.
- *Improved Collaboration:* Clear workflows and communication protocols enhanced coordination between surgeons, OR staff, and CSPD teams.

Financial Impact

- **Cost Savings:** Reduced unused supplies and non-value-added work resulted in annual savings of approximately $250,000 across the pilot locations.
- **Revenue Opportunities:** Improve OR efficiency allowed for increased case volumes, adding an estimated $400,000 in annual revenue.

Key Learnings

- **Importance of Standardization:** Creating a uniform process for preference card management ensured consistency across facilities and reduced errors.
- **Engaging Stakeholders:** Active involvement of surgeons and perioperative staff in the review and update process fostered buy-in and improved outcomes.
- **Data-Driven Decision-Making:** Using data analytics to identify high-use cards and monitor waste metrics enabled targeted interventions and measurable improvements.
- **Ongoing Review and Validation:** A six-month review cycle ensured that preference cards remained accurate and relevant, minimizing time wasted.

Replicability and Scalability

The success of the pilot demonstrated the feasibility of expanding the initiative systemwide.

Key steps for replicating and scaling the model include:

- Implementing standardized workflows across all facilities.
- Leveraging technology to streamline preference card updates and track utilization.
- Establishing continuous feedback loops to maintain accuracy and alignment with surgeon preferences.

Conclusion

This case study highlights the transformative potential of optimizing surgical preference card management. The health system achieved significant operational and financial benefits by addressing inefficiencies, reducing waste, and enhancing collaboration while improving staff satisfaction and patient outcomes. This initiative is a model for other organizations seeking to improve OR efficiency and streamline perioperative workflows.

CHECKLIST FOR ADDRESSING FIRST CASE AND TURNOVER DELAYS

Purpose: This checklist identifies and addresses common factors contributing to delays in first-case starts and OR turnover times and are designed to help OR teams quickly identify issues and implement solutions.

How to Use This Checklist

- Review this checklist before the first case of the day and between surgeries to ensure readiness.

- Assign responsibility to team members for each area.

- Document recurring issues and develop action plans to address them.

- Use this checklist as part of your ongoing quality improvement initiatives.

Personnel-Related Challenges

- [ ] Surgeon's delayed arrival
- [ ] Late arrival of the anesthesia team
- [ ] Unavailability or failure to schedule interpreter services
- [ ] Absence of surgical residents or physician assistants
- [ ] Pre-op nursing staff unprepared or unavailable
- [ ] Transport team delays or miscommunication
- [ ] Lack of orientation for new staff on specific protocols
- [ ] Unavailability of biomedical technician
- [ ] Unavailability of external contracted workforce

Documentation and Preparation Gaps

- [ ] Missing or incomplete patient consent forms.
- [ ] Incomplete or outdated patient history and physical records.
- [ ] Pre-operative assessments are either not completed or unavailable.
- [ ] Lack of pre-procedure directives or orders.
- [ ] Delayed or incomplete administrative paperwork.
- [ ] Incorrect or missing consent forms for specific procedures.
- [ ] Errors in documenting critical patient information.

Communication Breakdowns
- ☐ Difficulty locating attending surgeons.
- ☐ Scheduling conflicts with patients in other departments.
- ☐ Required staff unavailable on the OR schedule.
- ☐ Patients requesting last-minute clarifications from surgeons.
- ☐ Lengthy phone communications with the OR setup team.
- ☐ Patients failing to follow pre-op instructions.
- ☐ Miscommunication among team members regarding case details.

Process and Method Issues
- ☐ Delays caused by invasive procedures (e.g., line placements).
- ☐ Missing or incomplete consent forms for procedures requiring anesthesia.
- ☐ Variability in pre-op assessments conducted by nursing staff.
- ☐ Multiple team members ask patients for the same information.
- ☐ Scheduling errors for OR rooms or equipment.
- ☐ Blood products are not prepped or available when needed.

Environment and Setup Delays

- [ ] The operating room was not cleaned or prepped in time.
- [ ] Supplies, tools, or equipment are unavailable or unclean.
- [ ] Incorrect assembly of surgical kits.
- [ ] Broken or damaged instruments cause delays.
- [ ] Vendor support is unavailable for equipment repairs or replacements.

Material and Supply Issues

- [ ] Missing or inaccurate surgical preference lists.
- [ ] Incomplete kits or improperly assembled materials.
- [ ] Missing shared equipment or specialized instruments.
- [ ] Delays in obtaining sterilized tools or items.

Patient-Specific Issues

- [ ] Patients arriving at the wrong locations or without necessary support.
- [ ] Patients are not prepared physically or mentally for the procedure.
- [ ] Special considerations for pediatric, elderly, or incarcerated patients.
- [ ] Communication barriers (language, hearing, cognitive challenges).

Equipment Challenges

- [ ] Equipment malfunction or delays in setup.
- [ ] Competing demand for the same equipment in multiple rooms.
- [ ] Improper functioning of critical OR tools or technology.

ADDITIONAL
OR CHECKLIST

OR Efficiency Improvement Checklist

Purpose: A high-level checklist to evaluate areas for improvement in operating room efficiency.

- [ ] Turnover time is monitored and meets benchmarks (e.g., <30 minutes).
- [ ] First-case start times meet daily goals (>90% on-time starts).
- [ ] All staff receive orientation and training on standardized protocols.
- [ ] Conduct daily huddles to review case schedules and potential delays.
- [ ] Equipment and instruments are prepped and checked before cases.
- [ ] Preference cards are updated and standardized across surgeons.
- [ ] Key performance indicators (KPIs) are reviewed monthly for improvement.
- [ ] Lean processes reduce waste (e.g., motion, waiting time).

Leadership Rounding Checklist for OR Teams

Purpose: Helps leaders engage with OR staff and identify pain points.

- [ ] Conduct daily or weekly rounds to meet with OR staff.
- [ ] Ask staff about barriers to completing their work efficiently.
- [ ] Discuss recent delays or challenges and identify root causes.
- [ ] Recognize staff contributions and celebrate small wins.
- [ ] Review key OR performance metrics with staff.
- [ ] Provide updates on upcoming initiatives or changes.

Patient Preparation Checklist

Purpose: Ensures patients are ready for surgery to prevent delays.

- [ ] Consent forms are signed and verified for accuracy.
- [ ] Pre-op assessments are completed and documented.
- [ ] Patients have followed fasting instructions (e.g., NPO status).
- [ ] Interpreter services are scheduled (if applicable).
- [ ] Pre-op labs and imaging results are available in the chart.
- [ ] Special equipment (e.g., implants) is confirmed and ready.

Equipment Readiness Checklist

Purpose: Prevents equipment-related delays.

- ☐ Surgical instruments are sterilized and available for all cases.
- ☐ Test all the required equipment to ensure proper functioning (e.g., lights, monitors).
- ☐ Confirm vendor support for specialized equipment.
- ☐ Spare equipment is available in case of malfunction.
- ☐ Count instruments and verify before surgery begins.

Scheduling Optimization Checklist

Purpose: Ensures efficient scheduling to maximize OR utilization.

- ☐ Assign all cases to the appropriate OR with the correct resources.
- ☐ Block schedules are reviewed monthly and optimized for demand.
- ☐ Account for urgent and emergent cases without disrupting the routine schedule.
- ☐ Alignment of equipment and staffing with the appropriate case mix.
- ☐ Notify patients of their surgery time in advance.

FINANCIAL ANALYSIS TOOL

Financial Analysis Tool

Purpose: Helps OR managers assess cost efficiency and savings.

Metrics to Monitor:

- Cost per case.
- Turnover time costs (e.g., savings from reducing delays).
- Equipment utilization rates.
- Vendor pricing for surgical tools and supplies.
- Overtime expenses related to OR staff.

KPI Dashboard for OR Efficiency

Purpose: Tracks and visualizes key performance indicators for OR performance.

KPI Categories:

- Operational Metrics: On-time starts, turnover time, cases per day.
- Financial Metrics: Cost per case, revenue per OR day.
- Staff Metrics: Overtime hours, staff satisfaction scores.
- Patient Metrics: Surgical wait times, patient satisfaction scores.

Vendor and Contract Management Checklist

Purpose: Helps ensure smooth coordination with external vendors.

- Contracts are up-to-date and reviewed annually.
- Schedule vendor representatives for critical equipment setup or repairs.
- Identify backup vendors for emergencies.
- Supplies and implants are delivered on time and meet quality standards.

ABOUT THE AUTHOR

Sumit Sharma is a results-driven healthcare executive with over 20 years of experience in strategy, operational excellence, and innovation. As an executive leader in healthcare, Sumit leads growth strategy for Surgery and Digestive Health at one of the largest healthcare systems in the U.S., where he designs and implements transformative programs that enhance patient care, optimize workflows, and drive organizational growth.

Sumit is a recognized thought leader in healthcare strategy and market development, holding memberships with the Society for Health Care Strategy & Market Development (SHSMD), American College of Healthcare Executives (ACHE), Institute for Healthcare Improvement (IHI), and American Society for Gastrointestinal Endoscopy (ASGE). He was honored with the HFMA Phoenix Award 2024 for his exceptional contributions to healthcare. Sumit is also a certified Six Sigma Master Black Belt (SSMBB) and a Stanford Certified Project Manager (SCPM), underscoring his expertise in process improvement and project implementation.

In addition, Sumit holds four advanced certifications:
- Healthcare Financial Management Association (HFMA)
- Certified Revenue Cycle Representative (CRCR)
- Certified Healthcare Financial Professional (CHFP)
- Certificate of Strategy and Business Intelligence (CSBI)
- Certified Specialist Physician Practice Management (CSPPM)

Sumit has gained unparalleled insights into surgical workflows with hands-on experience observing and analyzing over 200 surgeries across inpatient operating rooms, outpatient surgery centers, ambulatory surgery centers, and endoscopy units. His expertise spans robotic-assisted, laparoscopic, and open procedures, empowering him to develop scalable, data-driven solutions that address the complex needs of clinical and operational teams. Before transitioning to healthcare, Sumit served as Head of Process Improvement and Growth Strategy at a Fortune 500 company, where he led enterprise-wide initiatives that delivered measurable efficiencies and significant business growth.

Sumit is also the author of Healthcare Perspective, a LinkedIn newsletter with over 1,700 subscribers, where he shares insights on healthcare transformation, leadership, and OR efficiency. His work has been featured in publications for the ACHE Arizona Chapter, fostering nationwide discussions among healthcare professionals.

Through his books, workshops, and thought leadership, Sumit remains committed to advancing healthcare delivery and empowering organizations to create more efficient, patient-centered systems.

www.ingramcontent.com/pod-product-compliance
Lightning Source LLC
Chambersburg PA
CBHW052126270326
41930CB00012B/2780